CU00657707

History of the Literature of Ancient Greece [Tr. by Sir G.C. Lewis and J.W. Donaldson].

Carl Otfried Müller

Nabu Public Domain Reprints:

You are holding a reproduction of an original work published before 1923 that is in the public domain in the United States of America, and possibly other countries. You may freely copy and distribute this work as no entity (individual or corporate) has a copyright on the body of the work. This book may contain prior copyright references, and library stamps (as most of these works were scanned from library copies). These have been scanned and retained as part of the historical artifact.

This book may have occasional imperfections such as missing or blurred pages, poor pictures, errant marks, etc. that were either part of the original artifact, or were introduced by the scanning process. We believe this work is culturally important, and despite the imperfections, have elected to bring it back into print as part of our continuing commitment to the preservation of printed works worldwide. We appreciate your understanding of the imperfections in the preservation process, and hope you enjoy this valuable book.

LIBRARY OF USEFUL KNOWLEDGE.

HISTORY OF THE
LITERATURE OF GREECE.
VOL. II.—PART I.

COMMITTEE.

Chairman—The Right Hon. LORD BROUGHAM, F.R.S., Member of the National Institute of France.
Vice Chairman—JOHN WOOD, Esq.
Treasurer—WILLIAM TOOKE, Esq., F.R.S.

ALFRED AINGER, Esq.
WM. ALLEN, Esq., F.R. and R.A.S.
CAPTAIN BEAUFORT, R.N. F.R. and R.A.S.
GEORGE BIRKBECK, M.D.
GEORGE BURROWS, M.D.
PETER STAFFORD CAREY, Esq., A.M.
JOHN CONOLLY, M.D.
WILLIAM COULSON, Esq.
R. DAVIS CRAIG, Esq.
J. F. DAVIS, Esq., F.R.S.
H. T. DE LA BECHE, Esq., F.R.S.
THE RIGHT HON. LORD DENMAN.
SAMUEL DUCKWORTH, Esq.
THE RIGHT REV. THE BISHOP OF DURHAM, D.D.
SIR HY. ELLIS, Prin. Lib. Brit. Mus.
T. F. ELLIS, Esq., A.M., F.R.A.S.
JOHN ELLIOTSON, M.D., F.R.S.
GEORGE EVANS, Esq., M.P.
THOMAS FALCONER, Esq.
I. L. GOLDSMID, Esq., F.R. and R.A.S.
FRANCIS HENRY GOLDSMID, Esq.
B. GOMPERTZ, Esq., F.R. and R.A.S.
J. T. GRAVES, Esq., A.M., F.R.S.
G. B. GREENOUGH, Esq., F.R. and L.S.
M. D. HILL, Esq., Q.C.
ROWLAND HILL, Esq., F.R.A.S.
RIGHT HON. SIR J. C. HOBHOUSE, Bart., M.P.
T. HODGKIN, M.D.
DAVID JARDINE, Esq., A.M.
HENRY B. KER, Esq.

THOMAS HEWITT KEY, Esq., A.M.
SIR CHARLES LEMON, Bart., M.P.
GEORGE C. LEWIS, Esq., A.M.
THOMAS HENRY LISTER, Esq.
JAMES LOCH, Esq., M.P., F.G.S.
GEORGE LONG, Esq., A.M.
HY. MALDEN, Esq, A.M.
ARTHUR T. MALKIN, Esq., A.M.
MR. SERJEANT MANNING.
R. I. MURCHISON, Esq., F.R.S., F.G.S.
THE RIGHT HON. LORD NUGENT.
W. SMITH O'BRIEN, Esq., M.P.
THE RIGHT HON. SIR HY. PARNELL, Bart., M.P.
RICHARD QUAIN, Esq.
P. M. ROGET, M.D., Sec. R.S., F.R.A.S.
EDWARD ROMILLY, Esq., A.M.
R. W. ROTHMAN, Esq., A.M.
THE RIGHT HON. LORD JOHN RUSSELL, M.P.
SIR MARTIN A. SHEE, P.R.A., F.R.S.
THE RIGHT HON. EARL SPENCER.
SIR GEO. T. STAUNTON, Bart., M.P.
JOHN TAYLOR, Esq., F.R.S.
A. T. THOMSON, M.D.
THOMAS VARDON, Esq.
JAMES WALKER, Esq., F.R.S.
HY. WAYMOUTH, Esq.
THOS. WEBSTER, Esq., A.M.
J. WHISHAW, Esq., A.M. F.R.S.
THE HON. JOHN WROTTESLEY, A.M., F.R.A.S.
JOHN ASHTON YATES, Esq., M.P.

THOMAS COATES, Esq., *Secretary*, 59, Lincoln's Inn Fields.

LONDON:
PUBLISHED BY THE SOCIETY FOR THE DIFFUSION OF USEFUL KNOWLEDGE,
59, LINCOLN'S INN FIELDS.

No. 325.]   *April 1, 1840.*   [*Price Sixpence.*

UNDER THE SUPERINTENDENCE OF THE SOCIETY FOR THE DIFFUSION
OF USEFUL KNOWLEDGE.

The publication of the Treatise of MINERALOGY is unavoidably
deferred.

POLITICAL PHILOSOPHY.

On the 20th of February was published, at the Society's Office, the First
Number of the Political Series, being a

PRELIMINARY DISCOURSE of the OBJECTS, PLEASURES,
and ADVANTAGES of POLITICAL SCIENCE;

and on the 16th of March was published No. II., being a Lecture on the

PRINCIPLES OF GOVERNMENT.

The succeeding Numbers will appear on the 15th of every Month.

For a Prospectus of the Series, see pages 3 and 4 of this Wrapper.

SECOND PERIOD

OF

GREEK LITERATURE

(Continued.)

CHAPTER XXVII.

§ 1. HAVING followed one species of the drama, *Tragedy*, through its rise, progress, and decay, up to the time when it almost ceases to be poetry, we must return once more to its origin, in order to consider how it came to pass that the other species, *Comedy*, though it sprang from the same causes, and was matured by the same vivifying influences, nevertheless acquired so dissimilar a form.

The opposition between tragedy and comedy did not make its first appearance along with these different species of the drama : it is as old as poetry itself. By the side of the noble and the great, the common and the base always appear in the guise of folly, and thus make the opposed qualities more conspicuous. Nay more, in the same proportion as the mind nurtured and cultivated within itself its conceptions of the perfect order, beauty, and power, reigning in the universe and exhibiting themselves in the life of man, so much the more capable and competent would it become to comprehend the weak and perverted in their whole nature and manner, and to penetrate to their very heart and centre. In themselves the base and the perverted are certainly no proper subject for poetry : when, however, they are received among the conceptions of a mind teeming with thoughts of the great and the beautiful, they obtain a place in the world of the beautiful and become poetic. In consequence of the conditional and limited existence of our

B

race, this tendency of the mind is always conversant about bare realities, while the opposite one has, with free creative energy, set up for itself a peculiar domain of the imagination. Real life has always furnished superabundant materials for comic poetry; and if the poet in working up these materials has often made use of figures which do not actually exist, these are always intended to represent actual appearances, circumstances, men, and classes of men: the base and the perverted are not invented; the invention consists in bringing them to light in their true form. A chief instrument of comic representation is *Wit*, which may be defined to be,—a startling detection and display of the perverted and deformed, when the base and the ridiculous are suddenly illuminated by the flash of genius. Wit cannot lay hold of that which is really sacred, sublime, and beautiful: in a certain sense, it invariably degrades what it handles; but it cannot perform this office unless it takes up a higher and safer ground from which to hurl its darts. Even the commonest sort of wit, which is directed against the petty follies and mistakes of social life, must have for its basis a consciousness of the possession of that discreet reserve and elegant refinement which constitute good manners. The more concealed the perversity, the more it assumes the garb of the right and the excellent; so much the more comic is it when ... seen through and detected, just because it is thus brought most ... uptly into contrast with the true and the good.

We must now break off these general considerations, which do not properly belong to the problem we have to solve, and are only designed to call attention to the cognate and corresponding features of tragic and comic poetry. If we return to history, we meet with the comic element even in *epic* poetry, partly in connexion with the heroic epos, where, as might be expected, it makes its appearance only in certain passages,* and partly cultivated in a separate form, as in the Margites. Lyric poetry had produced in the iambics of Archilochus masterpieces of passionate invective and derision, the form and matter of which had the greatest influence on dramatic comedy. It was not, however, till this dramatic comedy appeared, that wit and ridicule attained to that greatness of form, that unconstrained freedom, and, if we may so say, that inspired energy in the representation of the common and contemptible which every friend of antiquity identifies with the name of Aristophanes. At that happy epoch, when the full strength of the national

---

* As in the episode of Thersites and the comic scene with Agamemnon, above, chap. V. § 8. The Odyssey has more elements of the satyric drama (as in the story of Polyphemus) than of the comedy proper. Satyric poetry brings rude, unintellectual, half-bestial humanity into contact with the tragical; it places by the lofty forms of the heroes not human perverseness, but the want of real humanity, whereas comedy is conversant about the deterioration of civilized humanity. With regard to Hesiod's comic vein, see above chap. XI. § 3.; and for the Margites, the same chap. § 4.

ideas and the warmth of noble feelings were still united with the sagacious, refined, and penetrating observation of human life, for which the Athenians were invariably distinguished among the other Greeks. Attic genius here found the form in which it could not merely point out the depraved and the foolish as they appeared in individuals, but even grasp and subdue them when gathered together in masses, and follow them into the secret places where the perverted tendencies of the age were fabricated.

It was the *worship of Bacchus* again which rendered the construction of these great forms possible. It was by means of it that the imagination derived that bolder energy to which we have already ascribed the origin of the drama in general. The nearer the Attic comedy stands to its origin, the more it has of that peculiar inebriety of mind which the Greeks showed in everything relating to Bacchus; in their dances, their songs, their mimicry, and their sculpture. The unrestrained enjoyments of the Bacchic festivals imparted to all the motions of comedy a sort of grotesque boldness and mock dignity which raised to the region of poetry even what was vulgar and common in the representation: at the same time, this festal jollity of comedy at once broke through the restraints of decent behaviour and morality which, on other occasions, were strictly attended to in those days. " Let him stand out of the way of our choruses," cries Aristophanes,* " who has not been initiated into the Bacchic mysteries of the steer-eating Cratinus." The great comedian gives this epithet to his predecessor in order to compare him with Bacchus himself. A later writer regards comedy as altogether a product of the drunkenness, stupefaction, and wantonness of the nocturnal Dionysia ;† and though this does not take into account the bitter and serious earnestness which so often forms a back-ground to its bold and unbridled fun, it nevertheless explains how comedy could throw aside the restraints usually imposed by the conventions of society. The whole was regarded as the wild drollery of an ancient carnival. When the period of universal inebriety and licensed frolic had passed away, all recollection of what had been seen and done was dismissed, save where the deeper earnestness of the comic poet had left a sting in the hearts of the more intelligent among the audience. ‡

§ 2. The side of the multifarious worship of Bacchus to which comedy attached itself, was naturally not the same as that to which the origin of tragedy was due. Tragedy, as we have seen, proceeded from the Lenæa, the winter feast of Bacchus, which awakened and fostered an

---

* *Frogs,* v. 356.

† Eunapius, *Vitæ Sophist.* p. 32, ed. Boissonade, who explains from this the representation of Socrates in the *Clouds.* During the comic contest the people kept eating and tippling ; the choruses had wine given to them as they went on and came off the stage. Philochorus in Athenæus, xi. p. 464 F.

‡ The σοφοί, who are opposed to the γιλῶντις. Aristoph. *Ecclesiaz.* 1155.

enthusiastic sympathy with the apparent sorrows of the god of nature.
But comedy was connected, according to universal tradition, with
the *lesser* or *country* Dionysia, (τὰ μικρὰ, τὰ κατ' ἄγρους Διονύσια,)
the concluding feast of the vintage, at which an exulting joy
over the inexhaustible exuberant riches of nature manifested itself
in wantonness and petulance of every kind.   In such a feast the *comus*
or Bacchanalian procession was a principal ingredient : it was, of course,
much less orderly and ceremonious than the comus at which Pindar's
Epinician odes were sung, (chap. XV. § 3. p. 221,) but very lively and
tumultuous, a varied mixture of the wild carouse, the noisy song, and
the drunken dance.   According to Athenian authorities, which connect
comedy at the country Dionysia immediately with the comus,* it is in-
dubitable that the meaning of the word comedy is " a comus song,"
although others, even in ancient times, describe it as " a village song,"†
not badly as far as the fact is concerned, but the etymology is manifestly
erroneous.

With the Bacchic comus, which turned a noisy festal banquet into a
boisterous procession of revellers, a custom was from the earliest times
connected, which was the first cause of the origin of comedy.   The
symbol of the productive power of nature was carried about by this band
of revellers, and a wild, jovial song was recited in honour of the god in
whom dwells this power of nature, namely, Bacchus himself or one of
his companions.   Such phallophoric or ithyphallic songs were customary
in various regions of Greece.   The ancients give us many hints about
the variegated garments, the coverings for the face, such as masks or
thick chaplets of flowers, and the processions and songs of these comus
singers. ‡   Aristophanes, in his *Acharnians*, gives a most vivid picture
of the Attic usages in this respect : in that play, the worthy Dicæopolis,
while war is raging around, alone peacefully celebrates the country
Dionysia on his own farm ; he has sacrificed with his slaves, and now
prepares for the sacred procession ; his daughter carries the basket as
canephorus ; behind her the slave holds the phallus aloft ; and, while
his wife regards the procession from the roof of the house, he himself
begins the phallus song, " O Phales, boon companion of Bacchus, thou
nightly reveller !" with that strange mixture of wantonness and serious
piety which was possible only in the elementary religions of the ancient
world.

* See the quotations chap. XXI. § 5. ὁ κῶμος καὶ οἱ κωμῳδοί. The feast of the great
or city Dionysia is thus described, but it is obvious that the connexion proceeded
from the country Dionysia.

† From κώμη.   The Peloponnesians, according to Aristotle, *Poet.* c. 3, used this
etymology to support their claim to the invention of comedy, because they called
villages κῶμαι, but the Athenians δῆμοι.

‡ Athenæus, xiv. p. 621, 2, and the lexicographers Hesychius and Suidas, in
various articles relating to the subject. Phallophori, Ithyphalli, Autokabdali,
Iambistæ, are the different names of these merryandrews.

It belonged especially to the ceremonies of this Bacchic feast that, after singing the song in honour of the god who was the leader of the frolic, the merry revellers found an object for their unrestrained petulance in whatever came first in their way, and overwhelmed the innocent spectators with a flood of witticisms, the boldness of which was justified by the festival itself. When the phallophori at Sicyon had come into the theatre with their motley garb, and had saluted Bacchus with a song, they turned to the spectators and jeered and flouted whomsoever they pleased. How intimately these jests were connected with the Bacchic song, and how essentially they belonged to it, may be seen very clearly from the chorus in the *Frogs* of Aristophanes. This chorus is supposed to consist of persons initiated at Eleusis, who celebrate the mystic Dionysus Iacchus as the author of festal delights and the guide to a life of bliss in the other world. But this Iacchus is also, as Dionysus, the god of comedy, and the jokes which were suitable to these initiated persons, as an expression of their freedom from all the troubles of this life, also belonged to the country Dionysia, and attained to their highest and boldest exercise in comedy : this justifies the poet in treating *the chorus of the Mystæ as merely a mask for the comic chorus*, and in making it speak and sing much that was suitable to the comic chorus alone, which it resembled in all the features of its appearance.* And thus it is quite in the spirit of the old original comedy that the chorus, after having in beautiful strains repeatedly celebrated Demeter and Iacchus, the god who has vouchsafed to them to dance and joke with impunity, directly after, and without any more immediate inducement, attacks an individual arbitrarily selected :—" Will ye, that we join in quizzing Archedemus ?" &c. †

§ 3. This old lyric comedy, which did not differ much either in origin or form from the Iambics of Archilochus, may have been sung in various districts of Greece, just as it maintained its ground in many places even after the development of the dramatic comedy.‡ By what gradations,

---

* See below, chap. XXVIII. § 10.

† When Aristotle says (*Poet.* 4) that comedy originated ἀπὸ τῶν ἐξαρχόντων τὰ φαλλικά, he alludes to these unpremeditated jokes, which the *leader* of the Phallus song might have produced.

‡ The existence of a lyrical tragedy and comedy, by the side of the dramatic, has been lately established chiefly by the aid of Bœotian inscriptions, (*Corpus Inscript. Græcar.* No. 1584,) though it has been violently controverted by others. But though we should set aside the interpretation of these Bœotian monuments, it appears even from Aristotle, *Poet.* 4, (τὰ φαλλικὰ ἃ ἔτι καὶ νῦν ἐν πολλαῖς τῶν πόλεων διαμίνει νομιζόμενα,) that the songs, from which the dramatic comedy arose, still maintained their ground, as the ἰθύφαλλοι also were danced in the orchestra at Athens in the time of the orators. Hyperides *apud Harpocrat.* v. Ἰθύφαλλοι. It is clear that the comedies of Antheus the Lindian were also of this kind, according to the expressions of Athenæus, (x. p. 445 ;) " he composed comedies and many other things in the form of poems, which he sang as leader to his fellow-revellers who bore the phallus with him."

however, dramatic comedy was developed, can only be inferred from
the form of this drama itself, which still retained much of its original
organization, and from the analogy of tragedy: for even the ancients
laboured under a great deficiency of special tradition and direct information with regard to the progress of this branch of the drama.
Aristotle says that comedy remained in obscurity at the first, because it
was not thought serious or important enough to merit much attention;
that it was not till late that the comic poet received a chorus from the
archon as a public matter; and that previously, the choral-dancers were
volunteers.* The *Icarians*, the inhabitants of a hamlet which, according to the tradition, was the first to receive Bacchus in that part of the
country, and doubtless celebrated the country Dionysia with particular
earnestness, claimed the honour of inventing comedy; it was here that
Susarion was said, for the first time, to have contended with a chorus of
Icarians, who had smeared their faces with wine-lees, (whence their
name, τρυγῳδοί, or " lee-singers,") in order to obtain the prize, a basket
of figs and a jar of wine. It is worth noticing, that Susarion is said
to have been properly not of Attica, but a Megarian of Tripodiscus.†
This statement is confirmed by various traditions and hints from the
ancients, from which we may infer that the Dorians of Megara were distinguished by a peculiar fondness for jest and ridicule, which produced
farcical entertainments full of jovial merriment and rude jokes. If we
consider, in addition to this, that the celebrated Sicilian comedian Epicharmus dwelt at Megara in Sicily, (a colony of the Megarians who
lived near the borders of Attica,) before he went to Syracuse, and that
the Sicilian Megarians, according to Aristotle, laid claim to the invention of comedy, as well as the neighbours of the Athenians, we must
believe that some peculiar sparks of wit were contained in this little
Dorian tribe, which, having fallen on the susceptible temperaments of
the other Dorians, and also of the common people of Attica, brought the
talent for comedy to a speedy development.

Susarion, however, who is said to have flourished in Solon's time,
about Ol. 50, somewhat earlier than Thespis,‡ stands quite alone
in Attica; a long time elapses before we hear of any further cultivation
of comedy by poets of eminence. This will not surprise us if we recol-
lect that this interval is filled up by the long tyranny of Peisistratus and
his sons, who would feel it due to their dignity and security not to allow
a comic chorus, even under the mask of Bacchic inebriety and merriment, to utter ribald jests against them before the assembled people of
Athens; as understood by the Athenians of those days, comedy could
not be brought to perfection save by republican freedom and equality.§

* *Poet.* 5. Comp. above, chap. XXIII. § 1.
† See Müller's *Dorians*, Book IV. ch. 7. § 1.
‡ Parian marble. Ep. 39.   § See above, ch. XX. § 3.

This was the reason why comedy continued so long an obscure amusement of noisy rustics, which no archon superintended, and which no particular poet was willing to avow: although, even in this modest retirement, it made some sudden advances, and developed completely its dramatic form. Consequently, the first of the eminent poets received it in a definite and tolerably complete form.* This poet was *Chionides*, whom Aristotle reckons the first of the Attic comedians, (omitting Myllus and some other comedians, though they also left their works in writing,) and of whom we are credibly informed † that he began to bring out plays eight years before the Persian war (Ol. 73, B.C. 488). He was followed by *Magnes*, also born in the Bacchic village Icaria, who for a long time delighted the Athenians with his cheerful and multifarious fictions. To the same age of comedy belongs *Ecphantides*, who was so little removed from the style of the Megarian farce, that he expressly remarked in one of his pieces,—" He was not bringing forward a song of the Megarian comedy ; he had grown ashamed of making his drama Megarian."‡

§ 4. The second period of comedy comprises poets who flourished just before and during the Peloponnesian war. *Cratinus* died Ol. 89, 2. B.C. 423, being then very old; he seems to have been not much younger than Æschylus, and occupies a corresponding place among the comic poets; all accounts of his dramas, however, relate to the latter years of his life; and all we can say of him is, that he was not afraid to attack Pericles in his comedies at a time when that statesman was in the height of his reputation and power.§ *Crates* raised himself, from being an actor in the plays of Cratinus, to the rank of a distinguished poet: a career common to him with several of the ancient comedians. *Telecleides* and *Hermippus* also belong to the comic poets of the time of Pericles. *Eupolis* did not begin to bring out comedies till after the beginning of the Peloponnesian war (Ol. 87, 3. B.C. 429); his career terminated with that war. *Aristophanes* made his first appearance under another name in Ol. 88, 1. B.C. 427, and under his own name, Ol. 88, 4. B.C. 424 ; he went on writing till Ol. 97, 4. B.C. 388. Among the contemporaries of this great comic poet, we have also *Phrynichus* (from Ol. 87, 3. B.C. 429); *Plato* (from Ol. 88, 1. B.C. 427 to Ol. 97,

---

* Aristot. *Poet.* 5. ἤδη δὲ σχήματά τινα αὐτῆς ἐχούσης οἱ λεγόμενοι αὐτῆς ποιηταὶ μνημονεύονται.

† Suidas, v. Χιωνίδης. Consequently, Aristotle, *Poet.* 3, (or, according to F. Ritter, a later interpreter,) must be in error when he places Chionides a good deal later than Epicharmus.

‡   Μεγαρικῆς
      κωμῳδίας ᾆσμ' οὐ δίειμ'· ᾐσχυνόμην
        τὸ δρᾶμα Μεγαρικὸν ποιεῖν.

According to the arrangement of this fragment, (quoted by Aspasius on Aristot. *Eth. Nic.* iv. 2,) by Meineke, *Historia Critica Comicorum Græcorum*, p. 22, which is undoubtedly the correct one.

§ As appears from the fragments referring to the Odeion and the long walls.

1. B.C. 391, or even longer); *Pherecrates* (who also flourished during the Peloponnesian war); *Ameipsias*, who was sometimes a successful rival of Aristophanes; *Leucon*, who also frequently contended with Aristophanes; *Diocles, Philyllius, Sannyrion, Strattis, Theopompus*, who flourished towards the end of the Peloponnesian war and subsequently, form the transition to the middle comedy of the Athenians.*

We content ourselves for the present with this brief chronological view of the comic poets of the time, because in some respects it is impossible to characterize these authors, and in others, this cannot be done till we have become better acquainted with Aristophanes, and are able to refer to the creations of this poet. Accordingly, we will take a comparative glance at some of the pieces of Cratinus, Eupolis, and some others, after we have considered the comedy of Aristophanes: but must remark here beforehand that it is infinitely more difficult to form a conception of a lost comedy from the title and some fragments, than it would be to deal similarly with a lost tragedy. In the latter, we have in the mythical foundation something on which we may depend, and by the conformation of which the edifice to be restored must be regulated; whereas comedy, with its greater originality, passes at once from one distant object to another, and unites things which seem to have no connexion with one another, so that it is impossible to follow its rapid movements merely by the help of some traces accidentally preserved.

§ 5. Before we turn to the works of Aristophanes, we must make ourselves acquainted with comedy in the same way that we have already done with tragedy, in order that the technical forms into which the poet had to cast his ideas and fancies may stand clearly and definitely before our eyes. These forms are partly the same as in the tragic drama,— as the locality and its permanent apparatus were also common to both; in other respects they are peculiar to comedy, and are intimately connected with its origin and development.

To begin with the locality, the stage and orchestra, and, on the whole, their meaning, were *common* to tragedy and comedy. The stage (*Proscenion*) is, in comedy also, not the inside of a house, but some open space, in the background of which, on the wall of the scene, were represented public and private buildings. Nay, it appeared to the ancients so utterly impossible to regard the scene as a room of a house, that even the *new* comedy, little as it had to do with actual public life, nevertheless for the sake of representation, as we have remarked above, (Chap. XXII. § 5,) made the scenes which it represents public: it endea-

---

* According to the researches of Meineke, *Hist. Crit. Com. Græcorum. Callias*, who lived before Strattis, was likewise a comedian: his γραμματικὴ τραγῳδία could not have been a serious tragedy, but must have been a joke; the object and occasion of it, however, cannot easily be guessed at. The old grammarians must have been joking when they asserted that Sophocles and Euripides imitated this γραμματικὴ τραγῳδία in some piece or other.

vours, with as little sacrifice of nature as it may, so to arrange all the conversations and events that they may take place in the street and at the house-doors. The generally political subjects of the *old* comedy rendered this much less difficult; and where it was absolutely necessary to represent an inner chamber of a house, they availed themselves of the resource of the Eccyclema.

Another point, *common* to tragedy and comedy, was the limited number of the actors, by whom all the parts were to be performed. According to an authority,[*] (on which, however, we cannot place perfect reliance,) Cratinus raised the number to three, and the scenes in most of the comedies of Aristophanes, as also in the plays of Sophocles and Euripides, can be performed by three actors only. The number of subordinate persons in comedy has made the change of parts more frequent and more varied. Thus, in the *Acharnians*, while the first player acted the part of Dicæopolis, the second and third actors had to undertake now the Herald and Amphitheus, then again the ambassador and Pseudartabas; subsequently the wife and daughter of Dicæopolis, Euripides, and Cephisophon; then the Megarian and the Sycophant, and the Bœotian and Nicarchus.[†] In other pieces, however, Aristophanes seems to have introduced a fourth actor (as Sophocles has done in the *Œdipus at Colonus*); the *Wasps*, for example, could hardly have been performed without four actors.[‡]

The use of masks and of a gay and striking costume was also *common* to tragedy and comedy; but the forms of the one and the other were totally different. To conclude from the hints furnished by Aristophanes, (for we have a great want of special information on the subject,) his comic actors must have been still more unlike the *histriones* of the new comedy, of Plautus and Terence; of whom we know, from some very valuable and instructive paintings in ancient manuscripts, that they adopted, on the whole, the costume of every day life, and that the form and mode of their tunics and palliums were the same as those of the actual personages whom they represented. The costume of Aristophanes' players must, on the other hand, have resembled rather the garb of the farcical actors whom we often see depicted on vases from Magna Græcia, namely, close-fitting jackets and trowsers striped with divers colours, which remind us of the modern Harlequin; to which were added great bellies and other disfigurations and appendages purposely extravagant and indecorous, the grotesque form being, at the most, but partially covered by a little mantle: then there were masks, the

---

[*] *Anonym. de Comedia*, p. xxxii. Comp. Aristot. *Poet.* 5.

[†] The little daughters, who are sold as pigs, were perhaps puppets; their *koï, koï,* and the other sounds they utter, were probably spoken behind the scenes as a *parascenion.*

[‡] In the Wasps, Philocleon, Bdelycleon, and the two slaves Xanthias and Sosias, are frequently on the stage at the same time as speaking persons.

features of which were exaggerated even to caricature, yet so that particular persons, when such were brought upon the stage, might at once
be recognized.   It is well known that Aristophanes found great difficulty in inducing the mask-makers (σκευοποιοὶ) to provide him with a
likeness of the universally dreaded demagogue, Cleon, whom he introduces in his *Knights*.   The costume of the chorus in a comedy of Aristophanes went farthest into the strange and fantastic.   His choruses
of birds, wasps, clouds, &c., must not of course be regarded as having
consisted of birds, wasps, &c. actually represented, but, as is clear from
numerous hints from the poet himself, of a mixture of the human form
with various appendages borrowed from the creatures we have mentioned;* and in this the poet allowed himself to give special promi-
nence to those parts of the mask which he was most concerned about,
and for which he had selected the mask : thus, for example, in the *Wasps*,
who are designed to represent the swarms of Athenian judges, the sting
was the chief attribute, as denoting the style with which the judges used
to mark down the number of their division in the wax-tablets ; these
waspish judges were introduced humming and buzzing up and down, now
thrusting out, and now drawing in an immense spit, which was attached
to them by way of a gigantic sting.   Ancient poetry was suited, by its
vivid plastic representations, to create a comic effect by the first sight of
its comic chorus and its various motions on the stage ; as in a play of
Aristophanes (the Γῆρας), some old men come on the stage, and casting
off their age in the form of a serpent's skin (which was also called
γῆρας), immediately after conducted themselves in the most riotous and
intemperate manner.

§ 6. Comedy had much that was peculiarly its own in the arrangement, the movements, and the songs of the chorus.   The authorities
agree in stating the number of persons in the comic chorus at twenty-
four : it is obvious that the complete chorus of the tragic tetralogy, (consisting of forty-eight persons,) was divided into two, and comedy kept
its moiety undivided.   Consequently, comedy, though in other respects
placed a good deal below tragedy, had, nevertheless, the advantage of a
more numerous chorus by this, that comedies were always represented
separately, and never in tetralogies ; whence it happened also, that the
comic poets were much less prolific in plays than the tragic.†   This
chorus, when it appeared in regular order, came on in rows of six persons, and as it entered the stage sang the *parodos*, which, however, was
never so long or so artificially constructed as it was in many tragedies.
Still less considerable were the *stasima*, which the chorus sings at the

* Like the Αἶοι with beasts' heads (Æsop's fables) in the picture described by
Philostratus. *Imagines*, I. 3.

† With all Aristophanes' long career, only 54 were attributed to him, of which
four were said to be spurious—consequently, he only wrote half as many plays as
Sophocles. Compare above, chap. XXIV. § 2.

end of the scene while the characters are changing their dress: they only serve to finish off the separate scenes, without attempting to awaken that collected thought and tranquillity of mind which the tragic stasima were designed to produce. Deficiencies of this kind in its choral songs, comedy compensated in a very peculiar manner by its *parabasis*.

The parabasis, which was an address of the chorus in the middle of the comedy, obviously originated in those phallic traits, to which the whole entertainment was due; it was not originally a constituent part of comedy, but improved and worked out according to rules of art. The chorus, which up to that point had kept its place between the thymele and the stage, and had stood with its face to the stage, made an evolution, and proceeded in files towards the *theatre*, in the narrower sense of the word; that is, towards the place of the spectators. This is the proper *parabasis*, which usually consisted of anapæstic tetrameters, occasionally mixed up with other long verses; it began with a short opening song, (in anapæstic or trochaic verse,) which was called *kommation*, and ended with a very long and protracted anapæstic system, which, from its trial of the breath, was called *pnigos* (also *makron*). In this parabasis the poet makes his chorus speak of his own poetical affairs, of the object and end of his productions, of his services to the state, of his relation to his rivals, and so forth. If the parabasis is complete, in the wider sense of the word, this is followed by a second piece, which is properly the main point, and to which the anapæsts only serve as an introduction. The chorus, namely, sings a lyrical poem, generally a song of praise in honour of some god, and then recites, in trochaic verses, (of which there should, regularly, be sixteen,) some joking complaint, some reproach against the city, some witty sally against the people, with more or less reference to the leading subject of the play: this is called the *epirrhema*, or "what is said in addition." Both pieces, the lyrical strophe and the epirrhema, are repeated antistrophically. It is clear, that the lyrical piece, with its antistrophe, arose from the phallic song; and the epirrhema, with its antepirrhema, from the gibes with which the chorus of revellers assailed the first persons they met. It was natural, as the parabasis came in the middle of the whole comedy, that, instead of these jests directed against individuals, a conception more significant, and more interesting to the public at large, should be substituted for them; while the gibes against individuals, suitable to the original nature of comedy, though without any reference to the connexion of the piece, might be put in the mouth of the chorus whenever occasion served.*

As the parabasis completely interrupts the action of the comic drama,

---

* Such parts are found in the *Acharnians*, v. 1143-1174, in the *Wasps*, 1265-1291, in the *Birds*, 1470-1493, 1553-1565, 1694-1705. We must not trouble ourselves with seeking a connexion between these verses and other parts. In fact, it needed but the slightest suggestion of the memory to occasion such sallies as these.

it could only be introduced at some especial pause; we find that Aristophanes is fond of introducing it at the point where the action, after all
sorts of hindrances and delays, has got so far that the crisis must ensue,
and it must be determined whether the end desired will be attained or
not. Such, however, is the laxity with which comedy treats all these
forms, that the parabasis may even be divided into two parts, and the
anapæstical introduction be separated from the choral song; * there
may even be a second parabasis, (but without the anapæstic march,) in
order to mark a second transition in the action of the piece.† Finally,
the parabasis may be omitted altogether, as Aristophanes, in his Lysistrata, (in which a double chorus, one part consisting of women, the
other of old men, sing so many singularly clever odes,) has entirely dis-
pensed with this address to the public.‡

§ 7. It is a sufficient definition of the comic style of dancing to mention that it was the *kordax*, i. e. a species of dance which no Athenian
could practise sober and unmasked without incurring a character for
the greatest shamelessness.§ Aristophanes takes great credit to himself
in his *Clouds* (which, with all its burlesque scenes, strives after a nobler
sort of comedy than his other pieces) for omitting the *kordax* in this
play, and for having laid aside some indecencies of costume.‖ Every
thing shows that comedy, in its outward appearance, had quite the
character of a farce, in which the sensual, or rather bestial, nature of
man was unreservedly brought forward, not by way of permission only,
but as a *law* and *rule*. So much the more astonishing, then, is the
high spirituality, the moral worth, with which the great comedians have
been able to inspire this wild pastime, without thereby subverting its
fundamental characteristics. Nay, if we compare with this old comedy
the later conformation of the middle and new comedy, with the latter of
which we are better acquainted, and which, with a more decent exterior,
nevertheless preaches a far laxer morality, and if we reflect on the corresponding productions of modern literature, we shall almost be induced to believe that the old rude comedy, which concealed nothing,
and was, in the representation of vulgar life, itself vulgar and bestial,
was better suited to an age which meant well to morality and religion,
and was more truly based on piety, than the more refined comedy, as it

* Thus in the *Peace*, and in the *Frogs*, where the first half of the parabasis has
coalesced with the parodos and the Iacchus-song, (of which see above, § 2.) As
Iacchus has been already praised in this first part, the lyrical strophes of the second
part (v. 675 foll.) do not contain any invocation of gods, and such like, but are full
of sarcasms about the demagogues Cleophon and Cleigenes. We find the same
deviation, and from the same reasons, in the second parabasis of the *Knights*.
† As in the *Knights*.
‡ The parabasis is wanting in the *Ecclesiazusæ* and the *Plutus*, for reasons which
are stated in chap. XXVIII. § 11.
§ Theophrast. *Charact.* 6. comp. Casaubon.
‖ Aristophanes, *Clouds*, 537 foll.

is called, which threw a veil over everything, and, though it made vice ludicrous, failed to render it detestable.*

To return, however, to the kordax, and to connect with it a remark on the rhythmical structure of comedy; we learn accidentally that the trochaic metre was also called kordax,† doubtless because trochaic verses were generally sung as an accompaniment to the kordax dances. The trochaic metre, which was invented along with the iambic by the old iambographers, had a sort of lightness and activity, but wanted the serious and impressive character of the iambus. It was especially appropriated to cheerful dances; ‡ even the trochaic tetrameter, which was not properly a lyrical metre, invited to motions like the dance. § The rhythmical structure of comedy was obviously for the most part built upon the foundation of the old iambic poetry, and was merely extended and enlarged much in the same way as the Æolian and Doric lyrical poetry was adapted to tragedy, namely, by lengthening the verses to systems, as they are called, by a frequent repetition of the same rhythm. The *asynartetic* verses, in particular, *i. e.* loose combinations of rhythms of different kinds, such as dactylic and trochaic, which may be regarded as forming a verse and also as different verses, belong only to the iambic and comic poetry; and in this, comedy, though it added several new inventions, was merely continuing the work of Archilochus. ‖

That the prevalent form of the dialogue should be the same in tragedy and comedy, namely, the *iambic trimeter*, was natural, notwithstanding the opposite character of the two kinds of poetry; for this common organ of dramatic colloquy was capable of the most various treatment, and was modified by the comic poets in a manner most suitable to their object. The avoidance of spondees, the congregation of short syllables, and the variety of the cæsuras, impart to the verse of comedy an extraordinary lightness and spirit, and the admixture of anapæsts in all feet but the last, opposed as this is to the fundamental form of the trimeter, proves that the careless, voluble recitation of comedy treated the long and short syllables with greater freedom than the tragic art permitted. In order to distinguish the different styles and tunes, comedy employed, besides the trimeter, a great variety of metres, which we must suppose were also distinguished by different sorts of gesticula-

---

* Plutarch, in his comparison of Aristophanes and Menander, (of which an epitome has been preserved,) expresses an entirely opposite opinion, but this is only a proof how very often the later writers of antiquity mistook the form for the substance.

† Aristotle, quoted by Quintilian, ix. 4. Cicero *Orat.* 57.

‡ Chap. XI. § 8, 22.

§ Aristophan. *Peace*, 324 foll.

‖ For the sake of brevity, we merely refer to Hephæstion, cap. xv. p. 83 foll. Gaisf. and Terentianus, v. 2243.

   Aristophanis ingens micat sollertia,
   Qui sæpe metris multiformibus novis
   Archilochon arte est æmulatus musica. Comp. above, chap. XI. § 8.

tion and delivery, such as the light trochaic tetrameter so well suited to the dance, the lively iambic tetrameter, and the anapæstic tetrameter, flaunting along in comic pathos, which had been used by Aristoxenus of Selinus, an old Sicilian poet, who lived before Epicharmus.

In all these things comedy was just as inventive and refined as tragedy. Aristophanes had the skill to convey by his rhythms sometimes the tone of romping merriment, at others that of festal dignity; and often in jest he would give to his verses and his words such a pomp of sound that we lament he is not in earnest. In reading his plays we are always impressed with the finest concord between form and meaning, between the tone of the speech and the character of the persons; as, for example, the old, hot-headed Acharnians admirably express their rude vigour and boisterous impetuosity in the Cretic metres which prevail in the choral songs of the piece.

But who could with a few words paint the peculiar instrument which comedy had formed for itself from the language of the day? It was based, on the whole, upon the common conversational language of the Athenians,—the Attic dialect, as it was current in their colloquial intercourse; comedy expresses this not only more purely than any other kind of poetry, but even more so than the old Attic prose:* but this every day colloquial language is an extraordinarily flexible and rich instrument, which not only contains in itself a fulness of the most energetic, vivid, pregnant and graceful forms of expression, but can even accommodate itself to the different species of language and style, the epic, the lyric, or the tragic; and, by this means, impart a special colouring to itself.† But, most of all, it gained a peculiar comic charm from its parodies of tragedy; here a word, a form slightly altered, or pronounced with the peculiar tragical accent, often sufficed to recal the recollection of a pathetic scene in some tragedy, and so to produce a ludicrous contrast.

---

* We only remind the reader that the connexions of consonants which distinguish Attic Greek from its mother dialect the Ionic, ττ for σσ, and ββ for ρς, occur every where in Aristophanes, and even in the fragments of Cratinus, but are not found in Thucydides any more than in the tragedians; although even Pericles is said to have used these un-Ionic forms on the bema. Eustathius on the *Iliad.* x. 385, p. 813. In other respects, too, the prose of Thucydides has far more epic and Ionic gravity and unction than the poetry of Aristophanes,—even in particular forms and expressions.

† Plutarch very justly remarks, (*Aristoph. et Menandri comp.* 1,) that the diction of Aristophanes contains all styles, from the tragic and pathetic (ὄγκος) to the vulgarisms of farce, (σπερμολογία καὶ φλυαρία;) but he is wrong in maintaining that Aristophanes assigned these modes of speaking to his characters arbitrarily and at random.

CHAPTER XXVIII.

§ 1. Events of the life of Aristophanes; the mode of his first appearance. § 2. His dramas: the *Dætaleis*; the *Babylonians*; § 3. the *Acharnians* analyzed; § 4. the *Knights*; § 5. the *Clouds*; § 6. the *Wasps*; § 7. the *Peace*; § 8. the *Birds*; § 9. the *Lysistrata*; *Thesmophoriazusæ*; § 10. the *Frogs*; § 11. the *Ecclesiazusæ*; the *second Plutus*. Transition to the middle comedy.

§ 1. ARISTOPHANES, the son of Philippus, was born at Athens about Ol. 82. B. C. 452.* We should know more about the events of his life had the works of his rivals been preserved; for it is natural to suppose that he was satirized in them, much in the same way as he has attacked Cratinus and Eupolis in his own comedies. As it is, we can only assert that he passed over to Ægina with his family, together with other Attic citizens, as a *Cleruchus* or colonist, when that island was cleared of its old inhabitants, and that he became possessed of some landed property there.†

The life of Aristophanes was so early devoted to the comic stage, that we cannot mistake a strong natural tendency on his part for this vocation. He brought out his first comedies at so early an age that he was prevented (if not by law, at all events by the conventions of society) from allowing them to appear under his own name. It is to be observed that at Athens the state gave itself no trouble to inquire who was really the author of a drama: this was no subject for an official examination; but the magistrate presiding over any Dionysian festival at which the people were to be entertained with new dramas,‡ gave any chorus-teacher who offered to instruct the chorus and actors for a new drama the authority for so doing, whenever he had the necessary confidence in him. The comic poets, as well as the tragic, were professedly chorus-teachers, ˙(χοροδιδάσκαλοι, or, as they specially called themselves, κωμῳδοδιδάσκαλοι;) and in all official proceedings, such as assigning and bestowing the prize, the state only inquired who had taught the chorus, and thereby

* It is clearly an exaggeration when the Schol. on the *Frogs*, 504, calls Aristophanes σχεδὸν μειρακίσκος, i. e. about 18 years old, when he first came forward as a dramatist. If such were the case, he would have been at his prime in his 20th year, and would have ceased to compose at the age of 56. In the pieces of Aristophanes we discern indications of advanced age, and we therefore assume that he was at least 25 years old at the time of his first appearance as a comic poet, (B.C. 427.)

† See Aristoph. *Acharn.* 652; *Vita Aristoph.* p. 14; Küster, and Theagenes quoted by the Schol. on Plat. Apol. p. 93, 8, (p. 331, Bekk.) The Acharnians was no doubt brought out by Callistratus; but it is clear that the passage quoted above referred the public to the poet himself, who was already well known to his audience.

‡ At the great Dionysia, the first archon; (ὁ ἄρχων as he was emphatically called;) at the Lenæa, the *basileus*, or king archon.

brought the new piece before the public. The comic poets likewise retained for a longer period a custom, which Sophocles was the first to discontinue on the tragic stage, that the poet and chorus-teacher should also appear as the *protagonist* or chief actor in his own piece. This will explain what Aristophanes says in the *parabasis* of the *Clouds*, that his muse at first exposed her children, because, as a maiden, she dared not acknowledge their birth, and that another damsel had taken them up as her own; while the public, which could not be long in recognizing the real author, had nobly brought up and educated the foundlings.* Aristophanes handed over his earlier pieces, and some of the later ones too, either to Philonides or to Callistratus, two chorus teachers, with whom he was intimate, and who were at the same time poets and actors; and these persons produced them on the stage. The ancient grammarians state that he transferred to Callistratus the political dramas, and to Philonides those which related to private life.† It was these persons who applied for the chorus from the archon, who produced the piece on the stage, and, if it was successful, received the prize, of which we have several examples in the didascaliæ; in fact, everything was done as if they had been the real authors, although the discriminating public could not have failed to discover whether the real author of the piece was the newly-risen genius of Aristophanes or the well-known and hacknied Callistratus.

§ 2. The ancients themselves did not know whether Philonides or Callistratus brought out the Dætaleis, the first of his plays, which was performed in Ol. 88, 1. B. c. 427.‡ The *Feasters*, who formed the chorus in this piece, were conceived as a company of revellers who had banqueted in a temple of Hercules, (in whose worship eating and drinking bore a prominent part,§) and were engaged in witnessing a contest between the old frugal and modest system of education and the frivolous and talkative education of modern times, in the persons of two young men, *Temperate* (σώφρων) and *Profligate* (καταπύγων.) Brother *Profligate* was represented, in a dialogue between him and his aged father, as a despiser of Homer, as accurately acquainted with legal expressions, (in order, of course, to employ them in pettifogging quibbles,) and as a zealous partizan of the sophist Thrasymachus, and of Alcibiades the leader of the frivolous youth of the day. ‖ In his riper years,

* Compare the *Knights*, 513, where he says that many considered he had too long abstained from χορὸν αἰτῶν καθ' ἱαυτόν. In the parabasis of the *Wasps*, he compares himself to a ventriloquist who had before spoken through others.

† So the *anonym. de comedia apud Küster.* The *Vita Aristophanis* has the contrary statement, but merely from an error, as is shown by various examples.

‡ *Schol.* on the *Clouds*, 531.

§ Müller's *Dorians*, II. 12. § 10.

‖ In the important fragment preservedʹby Galen Ἱπποκράτους γλῶσσαι *Prooemium;* which has been recently freed from some corruptions which disfigured it. See Dindorf *Aristoph. Fragmenta. Dætal.* I.

Aristophanes completed in the *Clouds* what he had attempted in this early play.

The second play of Aristophanes was the *Babylonians*, and was brought out Ol. 88, 2. B. C. 426, under the name of Callistratus. This was the first piece in which Aristophanes adopted the bold step of making the people themselves, in their public functions, and with their measures for ensuring the public good, the subject of his comedy. He takes credit to himself, in the parabasis of the *Acharnians*, for having detected the tricks which the Athenians allowed foreigners, and especially foreign ambassadors, to play upon them, by lending too willing an ear to their flatteries and misrepresentations. He also maintains that he has shown how democratic constitutions fall into the power of demagogues; and that he has thereby gained a great name with the allies, and, as he says, with humorous rhodomontade, at the court of the Great King himself. The name of the piece is obviously connected with this. We infer from the statements of the old grammarians,* that the Babylonians, who formed the chorus, were represented as common labourers in the mills, the lowest sort of slaves at Athens, who were branded and were forced to work in the mills by way of punishment; and that they passed themselves off as Babylonians, *i. e.* as ambassadors from Babylon.

By this it was presumed that Babylon had revolted against the great king, who was constantly at war with Athens; and Aristophanes thought that the credulous Athenians might easily be gulled into the belief of something of the kind. The play would therefore be nearly related to that scene in the *Acharnians*, in which the supposed ambassadors of the Persian monarch make their appearance, though the one cannot be considered as a mere repetition of the other. Of course, these fictitious Babylonians were represented as a cheat practised on the Athenian Demus by the demagogues, who were then (after the death of Pericles) at the head of affairs; and Aristophanes had made Cleon the chief butt for his witty attacks. This comedy was performed at the splendid festival of the great Dionysia, in the presence of the allies and a number of strangers who were then at Athens; and we may see, from Cleon's earnest endeavours to revenge himself on the poet, how severely the powerful demagogue smarted under the attack made upon him. He

---

* See especially Hesychius on the verse: Σαμίων ὁ δῆμος ὡς πολυγράμματος: " these are the words of one of the characters in Aristophanes," says Hesychius, " when he sees the *Babylonians from the mill*, being astonished at their appearance, and not knowing what to make of it." The verse was clearly spoken by some one, who was looking at the chorus without knowing what they were intended to represent, and who mistook them for Samians branded by Pericles, so that πολυγράμματος contains a direct allusion to the invention of letters by the Samians. That these Babylonians were intended to represent mill-slaves appears to stand in connexion with the fact that *Eucrates*, a demagogue powerful at that very time, possessed mills. (Aristoph. *Knights*, 254.) The piece, however, seems to have been directed chiefly against Cleon.

dragged Callistratus* before the council of the Five Hundred, (which, as
a supreme tribunal, had also the superintendence of the festival amuse-
ments,) and overwhelmed him with reproaches and threats.   With regard to Aristophanes himself, it is probable that Cleon made an indirect
attempt to bring him into danger by an indictment against him for assuming the rights of a citizen without being entitled to them, (γραφὴ
ξενίας.)   There is no doubt that the poet successfully repelled the
charge, and victoriously asserted his civic rights.†

§ 3. In the following year, (Ol. 88, 3. B. c. 425,) at the Lenæa,
Aristophanes brought out the *Acharnians*, the earliest of his extant
dramas.   Compared with most of his plays, the *Acharnians* is a harmless piece : its chief object is to depict the earnest longing for a peaceful
country life on the part of those Athenians who took no pleasure in the
babbling of the market-place, and had been driven into the city against
their will by the military plans of Pericles.   Along with this, a few
lashes are administered to the demagogues, who, like Cleon, had inflamed
the martial propensities of the people, and to the generals, who, like
Lamáchus, had shown far too great a love for the war.   We have also in
this play an early specimen of his literary criticism, directed against
Euripides, whose overwrought attempts to move the feelings, and the
vulgar shrewdness with which he had invested the old heroes, were
highly offensive to our poet.   In this play we have at once all the peculiar characteristics of the Aristophanic comedy ;—his bold and genial originality, the lavish abundance of highly comic scenes with which he
has filled every part of his piece, the surprising and striking delineation
of character which expresses a great deal with a few master-touches,
the vivid and plastic power with which the scenes are arranged, the ease
with which he has disposed of all difficulties of space and time.   Indeed, the play possesses its author's peculiar characteristics in such
perfection and completeness, that it may be proper in this place to give
such an analysis of this, *the oldest extant comedy*, as may serve to illustrate not merely the general ideas, which we have already given, but
also the whole plot and technical arrangement of the drama.

The stage in this play represents sometimes town and sometimes
country, and was probably so arranged that both were shown upon it at
once.   When the comedy begins, the stage gives us a glimpse of the
Pnyx, or place of public assembly ; that is to say, the spectator saw the

---

*We say *Callistratus*, because, as χοροδιδάσκαλος and protagonist in the *Acharnians*,
he acted the part of Dicæopolis, and because the public could not fail to understand
the words αὐτός τ᾽ ἐμαυτὸν ὑπὸ Κλέωνος ἃ ᾽παθον, ἐπίσταμαι, v. 377 foll., as spoken of
the performer himself.   In the ποιητής of the *parabasis* in the *Acharnians* we do not
hesitate to recognize Aristophanes, whose talents could not have remained unknown
to the public for three years.
   † *Schol. Acharn.* 377.   It was on this occasion, according to the author of the
Vita Aristophanis, that Aristophanes quoted that verse of Homer, (*Odyss.* I. 216,)
οὐ γάρ πώ τις ἑὸν γόνον αὐτὸς ἀνέγνω.

bema for the orator cut out of the rock, and around it some seats and other objects calculated to recal the recollection of the well-known place. Here sits the worthy Dicæopolis, a citizen of the old school, grumbling about his fellow citizens, who do not come punctually to the Pnyx, but lounge idly about the market-place, which is seen from thence; for his own part, although he has no love for a town-life, with its bustle and gossip, he attends the assembly regularly in order to speak for peace. On a sudden the Prytanes come out of the council-house; the people rush in; a well-born Athenian, Amphitheus, who boasts of having been destined by the gods to conclude a peace with Sparta, is dismissed with the utmost contempt, in spite of the efforts of Dicæopolis on his behalf; and then, to the great delight of the war party, ambassadors are introduced, who have returned from Persia, and have brought with them a Persian messenger, " the Great King's eye," with his retinue: this forms a fantastic procession, which, as Aristophanes hints, is all a trick and imposture, got up by the demagogues of the war party. Other ambassadors bring a similar messenger from Sitalces, king of Thrace, on whose assistance the Athenians of the day built a great deal, and drag before the assembly a miserable rabble, under the name of picked Odomantian troops, which the Athenians are to take into their service for very high pay. Meanwhile Dicæopolis, seeing that he cannot turn affairs into another channel, has sent Amphitheus to Sparta on his own account; the messenger returns in a few minutes with various treaties, (some for a longer, others for a shorter time,) in the form of wine-jars, like those which were used for pouring out libations on the conclusion of a treaty of peace; Dicæopolis selects a thirty years' truce by sea and land, which does not smell of pitch and tar, like a short armistice in which there is only just time to calk the ships. All these delightful scenes are possible only in a comedy like that of the Athenians, which has its outward form for the representation of every relation, every function, and every character; which is able to sketch everything in bold colours by means of grotesque speaking figures, and does not trouble itself with confining the activity of these figures to the laws of reality and the probabilities of actual life.*

The first dramatic complication which Aristophanes introduces into his plot, arises from the chorus, which consists of *Acharnians,* i. e., the inhabitants of a large village of Attica, where the people gained a livelihood chiefly by charcoal-burning, the materials for which were supplied by the neighbouring mountain-forests: they are represented as rude,

---

* In all this, comedy does but follow in its own way the spirit of *ancient art* in general, which went far beyond modern art in finding an outward expression for every thought and feeling of the mind, but fell short of our art in keeping up an appearance of consistency in the employment of these forms, as the laws of actual life would have required.

robust old fellows, hearts of oak, martial by their disposition, and especially incensed against the Peloponnesians, who had destroyed all the vineyards in their first invasion of Attica.   These old Acharnians at first appear in pursuit of Amphitheus, who, they hear, has gone to Sparta to bring treaties of peace: in his stead, they fall in with Dicæopolis, who is engaged in celebrating the festival of the country Dionysia, here represented as an abstract of every sort of rustic merriment and jollity, from which the Athenians at that time were debarred. The chorus no sooner learns from the phallus-song of Dicæopolis, that he is the person who has sent for the treaties, than they fall upon him in the greatest rage, refuse to hear a word from him, and are going to stone him to death without the least compunction, when Dicæopolis seizes a charcoal-basket, and threatens to punish it as a hostage for all that the Acharnians do to himself.   The charcoal-basket, which the Acharnians needed for their every-day occupations, is so dear to their hearts that they are willing, for its sake, to listen to Dicæopolis; especially as he has promised to speak with his head on a block, on condition that he shall be beheaded at once if he fails in his defence.   All this is amusing enough in itself, but becomes additionally ludicrous when we remember that the whole of Dicæopolis's behaviour is an imitation of one of the heroes of Euripides, the rhetorical and plaintive Telephus, who snatched the infant Orestes from his cradle and threatened to put him to death, unless Agamemnon would listen to him, and was exposed to the same danger when he spoke before the Achæans as Dicæopolis is when he argues with the Acharnians.   Aristophanes pursues this parody still farther, as it furnishes him with the means of exaggerating the situation of Dicæopolis in a very comic manner ; Dicæopolis applies to Euripides himself, (who is shown to the spectators by means of an eccyclema, in his garret, surrounded by masks and costumes, such as he was fond of employing for his tragic heroes,) and begs of him the most piteous of his dresses, upon which he obtains the most deplorable of them all, that of Telephus.   We pass over other mockeries of Euripides, in which Aristophanes indulges from pure wantonness, and turn to the following scene, one of the chief scenes in the piece, in which Dicæopolis, in the character of a comic Telephus, and with his head over the block, pleads for peace with the Spartans. It is obvious, that however seriously Aristophanes embraced the cause of the peace-party, he does not on this occasion speak one word in serious earnest.   He derives the whole Peloponnesian war from a bold frolic on the part of some drunken young men, who had carried off a harlot from Megara, in reprisal for which the Megarians had seized on some of the attendants of Aspasia.   As this explanation is not satisfactory, and the chorus even summons to its assistance the warlike Lamachus, who rushes from his house in extravagant military costume,* Dicæopolis is driven to have recourse to *argumenta ad hominem*, and he impresses on the old people who form the chorus, that *they* are obliged to serve as common soldiers, while young braggadocios, like Lamachus, made a pretty livelihood by serving as generals or ambassadors, and so wasted the fat of the land. This produces its effect, and the chorus shows an inclination to do justice to Dicæopolis. This catastrophe of the piece is followed by the parabasis, in the first part of which the poet, with particular reference to his last play, takes credit to himself for being an estimable friend to the people; he says that he does not indeed spare them, but that they need not fear, for that he will be just in his satire.† The second part, however, keeps close to the thought which Dicæopolis had awakened in the minds of the chorus; they complain bitterly of the assumption of their rights by the clever, witty, and ready young men, from whom they could not defend themselves, especially in the law-courts.

The second part of the piece, after the catastrophe and parabasis, is merely a description, overflowing with wit and humour, of the blessings which peace has conferred on the sturdy Dicæopolis. At first he opens his free market, which is visited in succession by a poor starving wretch from Megara, (the neighbouring country to Attica, which, poorly gifted by nature, had suffered in the most shocking manner from the Athenian blockade and the yearly devastations of its territory,) and by a stout Bœotian from the fertile land on the shore of the Copaic lake, which was well known to the Athenians for its eels. For want of other wares, the Megarian has dressed up his little daughters like young pigs, and the honest Dicæopolis is willing to buy them as such, though he is strangely surprised by some of their peculiarities;—a purely ludicrous scene, which was based, perhaps, on the popular jokes of the Athenians; a Megarian would gladly sell his children as little pigs, if any one would take them off his hands:—we could point out many jokes of this kind in the popular life, as well of ancient as of modern times. During this, the dealers are much troubled by sycophants, a race who lived by indictments, and were especially active in hunting for violations of the customs' laws; ‡ they want to seize on the foreign goods as contraband, but Dicæopolis makes short work with them; one of the

---

* Consequently, the house was also represented on the stage; probably the town house of Dicæopolis was in the middle, on the one side that of Euripides, on the other that of Lamachus. On the left was the place which represented the Pnyx; on the right some indication of a country house: this, however, occurs only in the scene of the country Dionysia, all the rest takes place in the city.

† v. 655. ἀλλ' ὑμεῖς μή ποτε δεῖσθ' ὡς κωμῳδήσει τὰ δίκαια. When we find such open professions as this, we may at least be certain that Aristophanes *intended* to direct the sting of his comedy against that only which appeared to him to be really bad.

‡ The sycophants, no doubt, derived their names from a sort of φάσις, *i. e.* public information against those who injured the state in any of its pecuniary interests.

sycophants he drives away from his market; the other, the little Nicarchus, he binds up in a bundle, and packs him on the back of the Bœotian, who shows a desire to take him away as a laughable little monkey.

Now begins, on a sudden, the Athenian feast of the pitchers (the Χόες). Lamachus * in vain sends to Dicæopolis for some of his purchases, in order that he may keep the feast merrily; the good citizen keeps every thing to himself, and the chorus, which is now quite converted, admires the prudence of Dicæopolis, and the happiness he has gained by it. In the midst of his preparations for a sumptuous banquet, others beg for some share of his peace; he returns a gruff answer to a countryman whose cattle have been harried by the Bœotians; but he behaves a little more civilly to a bride who wants to keep her husband at home. Meanwhile, various messages are brought; to Lamachus, that he must march against the Bœotians, who are going to make an inroad into Attica at the time of the feast of the Choes; to Dicæopolis, that he must go to the priest of Bacchus, in order to assist him in celebrating the feast of the Choes. Aristophanes works out this contrast in a very amusing manner, by making Dicæopolis parody every word which Lamachus utters as he is preparing for war, so as to transfer it to his own festivities; and when, after a short time which the chorus fills up by a satirical song, Lamachus is brought back from the war wounded, and supported by two servants, Dicæopolis meets him in a happy state of intoxication, and leaning on two damsels of easy virtue, and so celebrates his triumph over the wounded warrior in a very conspicuous manner.

To say nothing of the pithy humour of the style, and the beautiful rhythms and happy turns of the choral songs, it must be allowed that this series of scenes has been devised with genial merriment from beginning to end, and that they must have produced a highly comic effect, especially if the scenery, costumes, dances, and music were worthy of the conceptions and language of the poet. The piece, if correctly understood, is nothing but a Bacchic revelry, full of farce and wantonness; for although the conception of it may rest upon a moral foundation, yet the author is, throughout the piece, utterly devoid of seriousness and sobriety, and in every representation, as well of the victorious as of the defeated party, follows the impulses of an unrestrained love of mirth. At most, Aristophanes expresses his own sentiments in the parabasis: in the other parts of the play we cannot safely recognize the opinions of the poet in the deceitful mirror of his comedy.

§ 4. The following year (Ol. 88, 4. B.C. 424) is distinguished in the

---

* That Lamachus is only a representative of the warlike spirits is clear from his name, Λα-μαχος: otherwise, Phormio, Demosthenes, Paches, and other Athenian heroes might just as well have been substituted for him.

history of comedy by the appearance of the *Knights* of Aristophanes. It was the first piece which Aristophanes brought out in his own name, and he was induced by peculiar circumstances to appear in it as an actor himself. This piece is entirely directed against Cleon; not, like the *Babylonians*, and at a later period the *Wasps*, against certain measures of his policy, but against his entire proceedings and influence as a demagogue. There is a certain degree of spirit in attacking, even under the protection of Bacchic revelry, a popular leader who was mighty by the very principle of his policy, viz. of advancing the material interests and immediate advantage of the great mass of the people at the sacrifice of every thing else; and who had become still more formidable by the system of terrorism with which he carried out his views. This system consisted in throwing all the citizens opposed to him under the suspicion of being concealed aristocrats; in the indictments which he brought against his enemies, and which his influence with the law courts enabled him without difficulty to turn to his own advantage; and in the terrible severity with which he urged the Athenians in the public assembly and in the courts to put down all movements hostile to the rule of the democracy, and of which his proposal to massacre the Mitylenæans is the most striking example. Besides, at the very time when Aristophanes composed the *Knights*, Cleon's reputation had attained its highest pitch, for fortune in her sport had realized his inconsiderate boast, that it would be an easy matter for him to capture the Spartans in Sphacteria; the triumph of having captured these formidable warriors, for which the best generals had contended in vain, had fallen, like an over-ripe fruit, into the lap of the unmilitary Cleon (in the summer of the year 425). That it really was a bold measure to attack the powerful demagogue at this time, may also be inferred from the statement that no one would make a mask of Cleon for the poet, and still less appear in the character of Cleon, so that Aristophanes was obliged to undertake the part himself.

The *Knights* is by far the most violent and angry production of the Aristophanic Muse; that which has most of the bitterness of Archilochus, and least of the harmless humour and riotous merriment of the Dionysia. In this instance comedy almost transgresses its proper limits; it is almost converted into an arena for political champions fighting for life and death; the most violent party animosity is combined with some obvious traces of personal irritation, which is justified by the judicial persecution of the author of the Babylonians. The piece presents a remarkable contrast to the Acharnians; just as if the poet wanted to show that a checkered variety of burlesque scenes was not necessary to his comedy, and that he could produce the most powerful effect by the simplest means; and doubtless, to an audience perfectly familiar with all the hints and allusions of the comedian, the Knights must have

possessed still greater interest than the Acharnians, though modern
readers, far removed from the times, have not been always able to
resist the feeling of tediousness produced by the prolix scenes' of
the piece.   The number of characters is small and unpretending;
the whole *dramatis personæ* consist of an old master with three
slaves, (one of whom, a Paphlagonian, completely governs his master,)
and a sausage-seller.   The old master, however, is the *Demus of
Athens*, the slaves are the Athenian generals *Nicias* and *Demosthenes*,
and the Paphlagonian is *Cleon*: the sausage-seller alone is a fiction of
the poet's,—a rude, uneducated, impudent fellow, from the dregs of the
people, who is set up against Cleon in order that he may, by his auda-
city, bawl down Cleon's impudence, and so drive the formidable demagogue out of the field in the only way that is possible.   Even the chorus
has nothing imaginary about it, but consists of the Knights of the
State,* *i.e.* of citizens who, according to Solon's classification, which still
subsisted, paid taxes according to the rating of a knight's property, and
most of whom at the same time still served as cavalry in time of war :†
being the most numerous portion of the wealthier and better educated
class, they could not fail to have a decided antipathy to Cleon, who
had put himself at the head of the mechanics and poorer people.
We see that in this piece Aristophanes lays all the stress on the
political tendency, and considers the comic plot rather as a form and
dress than as the body and primary part of his play.   The allegory,
which is obviously chosen only to cover the sharpness of the attack, is
cast over it only like a thin veil; according to his own pleasure, the
poet speaks of the affairs of the Demus sometimes as matters of family
arrangement, sometimes as public transactions.

The whole piece has the form of a contest.   The sausage-seller (in
whom an oracle, which has been stolen from the Paphlagonian while he
was sleeping, recognizes his victorious opponent) first measures his
strength against him in a display of impudence and rascality, by which
the poet assumes that of the qualities requisite to the demagogue these
are the most essential.   The sausage-seller narrates that having, while
a boy, stolen a piece of meat and boldly denied the theft, a statesman
had predicted that the city would one day trust itself to his guidance.
After the parabasis, the contest begins afresh; the rivals, who had in
the meantime endeavoured to recommend themselves to the council,

* Hardly of actual knights, so that in this case reality and the drama were one
and the same.   That no *phyle*, but the state paid the expenses of this chorus, (if we
are so to explain *ἐπμερία* in the didascalia of the piece : see the examples in Böckh's
Public Economy of Athens, book iii. § 22, at the end,) is no ground for the former
inference.

† That Aristophanes considers the knights as a *class* is pretty clear from their
known political tendency; as part *of the Athenian army*, he often describes them
as sturdy young men, fond of horsemanship, and dressed in grand military costume.

come before Demus himself, who takes his seat on the Pnyx, and sue for the favour of the childish old man. Combined with serious reproaches directed against Cleon's whole system of policy, we have a number of joking contrivances, as when the sausage-seller places a cushion under the Demus, in order that he may not gall that which sat by the oar at Salamis.* The contest at last turns upon the oracles, to which Cleon used to appeal in his public speeches, (and we know from Thucydides † how much the people were influenced throughout the Peloponnesian war by the oracles and predictions attributed to the ancient prophets;) in this department, too, the sausage-seller outbids his rival by producing announcements of the greatest comfort to the Demus, and ruin to his opponent. As a merry supplement to these long-spun transactions, we have a scene which must have been highly entertaining to eye and ear alike: the Paphlagonian and the sausage-seller sit down as eating-house keepers (κάπηλοι) at two tables, on which a number of hampers and eatables are set out, and bring one article after the other to the Demus with ludicrous recommendations of their excellences ;‡ in this, too, the sausage-seller of course pays his court to the Demus more successfully than his rival. After a second parabasis we see the Demus—whom the sausage-seller has restored to youth by boiling him in his kettle, as Medea did Æson—in youthful beauty, but attired in the old-fashioned splendid costume, shining with peace and contentment, and in his new state of mind heartily ashamed of his former absurdities.

§ 5. In the following year we find Aristophanes (after a fresh suit § in which Cleon had involved him) bringing out the *Clouds*, and so entering upon an entirely new field of comedy. He had himself made up his mind to take a new and peculiar flight with this piece. The public and the judges, however, determined otherwise; it was not Aristophanes but the aged Cratinus who obtained the first prize. The young poet, who had believed himself secure against such a slight, uttered some warm reproaches against the public in his next play; he was induced, however, by this decision to revise his piece, and it is this *rifaccimento* (which deviates considerably from the original form) that has come down to us.||

There is hardly any work of antiquity which it is so difficult to

---

* Ἵνα μὴ τρίβῃς τὴν ἐν Σαλαμῖνι. v. 785.   † Thucyd. ii. 54. viii. 1.

‡ The two eating houses are represented by an eccyclema, as is clear from the conclusion of the scene.

§ See the *Wasps*, v. 1284. According to the *Vita Aristoph.* the poet had to stand three suits from Cleon touching his rights as a citizen.

|| The first *Clouds* had, according to a definite tradition, a different *parabasis;* it wanted the contest of the δίκαιος and ἄδικος λόγος, and the burning of the school at the end. It is also probable, from Diog. Laërt. ii. 18, (notwithstanding all the confusions which he has made,) that, in the first Clouds, Socrates was brought into connexion with Euripides, and was declared to have had a share in the tragedies of the latter.

estimate as the *Clouds* of Aristophanes. Was Socrates really, perhaps only in the earlier part of his career, the fantastic dreamer and sceptical sophist which this piece makes him? And if it is certain that he was not, is not Aristophanes a common slanderer, a buffoon, who, in the vagaries of his humour, presumes to attack and revile even what is purest and noblest? Where remains his solemn promise never to make what was right the object of his comic satire?

If there be any way of justifying the character of Aristophanes, as it appears to us in all his dramas, even in this hostile encounter with the noblest of philosophers; we must not attempt, as some modern writers have done, to convert Aristophanes into a profound philosopher, opposed to Socrates; but we must be content to recognize in him, even on this occasion, the vigilant patriot, the well-meaning citizen of Athens, whose object it is by all the means in his power to promote the interests of his native country, so far as he is capable of understanding them.

As the piece in general is directed against the new system of education, we must first of all explain its nature and tendency. Up to the time of the Persian war, the school-education of the Greeks was limited to a very few subjects. From his seventh year, the boy was sent to schools in which he learned reading and writing, to play on the lute and sing, and the usual routine of gymnastic exercises.* In these schools it was customary to impress upon the youthful mind, in addition to these acquirements, the works of the poets, especially Homer, as the foundation of all Greek training, the religious and moral songs of the lyric poets, and a modest and decent behaviour. This instruction ceased when the youth was approaching to manhood; then the only means of gaining instruction was intercourse with older men, listening to what was said in the market-place, where the Greeks spent a large portion of the day, taking a part in' public life, the poetic contests, which were connected with the religious festivals, and made generally known so many works of genius; and, as far as bodily training was concerned, frequenting the gymnasia kept up at the public expense. Such was the method of education up to the Persian war; and no effect was produced upon it by the more ancient systems of philosophy, any more than by the historical writings of the period, for no one ever thought of seeking the elements of a regular education from Heraclitus or Pythagoras, but whoever applied himself to them did so for his life. With the Persian war, however, according to an important observation of Aristotle,† an entirely new striving after knowledge and education developed itself among the Greeks; and subjects of instruction were established, which soon exercised an important influence on the whole spirit and character of the

---

* ἱς γραμματιστοῦ, ἱς κιθαριστοῦ, ἱς παιδοτρίβου.   † Aristot. *Polit.* viii. 6.

nation. The art of speaking, which had hitherto afforded exercise only to practical life and its avocations, now became a subject of school-training, in connexion with various branches of knowledge, and with ideas and views of various kinds, such as seemed suitable to the design of guiding and ruling men by eloquence. All this taken together, constituted the lessons of the Sophists, which we shall contemplate more nearly hereafter; and which produced more important effects on the education and morals of the Greeks than anything else at that time. That the very principles of the sophists must have irritated an Athenian with the views and feelings of Aristophanes, and have at once produced a spirit of opposition, is sufficiently obvious: the new art of rhetoric, always eager for advantages, and especially when transferred to the dangerous ground of the Athenian democracy and the popular law-courts, could not fail to be regarded by Aristophanes as a perilous instrument in the hands of ambitious and selfish demagogues; he saw with a glance how the very foundations of the old morality, upon which the weal of Athens appeared to him to rest, must be sapped and rooted up by a stream of oratory which had the skill to turn everything to its own advantage. Accordingly, he makes repeated attacks on the whole race of the artificial orators and sceptical reasoners, and it is with them that he is principally concerned in the *Clouds*.

The real object of this piece is stated by the poet himself in the parabasis to the Wasps, which was composed in the following year: he says that he had attacked the fiend which, like a night-mare, plagued fathers and grandfathers by night, besetting inexperienced and harmless people with all sorts of pleadings and pettifogging tricks.* It is obvious that it is not the teachers of rhetoric who are alluded to here, but the young men who abused the facility of speaking which they had acquired in the schools by turning it to the ruin of their fellow citizens. The whole plan of the drama depends on this: an old Athenian, who is sore pressed by debts and duns, first labours to acquire a knowledge of the tricks and stratagems of the new rhetoric, and finding that he is too stiff and awkward for it, sends to this school his youthful son, who has hitherto spent his life in the ordinary avocations of a well-born cavalier. The consequence is, that his son, being initiated into the new scepticism, turns it against his own father, and not only beats him, but proves that he has done so justly. The error of Aristophanes in identifying the school of Socrates with that of the new-fangled rhetoric must have arisen from his putting Socrates on the same footing with sophists, like Protagoras and Gorgias, and then preferring to make his fellow citizen the butt of his witticisms, rather than his foreign colleagues, who paid only short visits to Athens. It cannot be denied that Aristophanes was mistaken.

* Compare, by way of explanation, also *Acharnians*, 713. *Birds*, 1347. *Frogs*, 147.

It must indeed be allowed that Socrates, in the earlier part of his career, had not advanced with that security with which we see him invested in the writings of Xenophon and Plato, that he still took more part in the speculations of the·Ionian philosophers with regard to the universe,* than he did at a later period; that certain wild elements were still mixed up in his theory, and not yet purged out of it by the Socratic dialectic: still it is quite inconceivable that Socrates should ever have kept a school of rhetoric (and this is the real question), in which instruction was given, as in those of the sophists, how to make the worse appear the better reason.† But even this misrepresentation on the part of Aristophanes may have been undesigned: we see from passages of his later comedies,‡ that he actually regarded Socrates as a rhetorician and declaimer. He was probably deceived by appearances into the belief that the *dialectic* of Socrates, the art of investigating the truth, was the same as the *sophistry* which aped it, and which was but the art of producing a deceitful resemblance of the truth. It is, no doubt, a serious reproach to Aristophanes that he did not take the trouble to distinguish more accurately between the two: but how often it happens that men, with the best intentions, condemn arbitrarily and in the lump those tendencies and exertions which they dislike or cannot appreciate.

The whole play of the *Clouds* is full of ingenious ideas, such as the *chorus of Clouds* itself, which Socrates invokes, and which represents appropriately the light, airy, and fleeting nature of the new philosophy.§ A number of popular jokes, such as generally attach themselves to the learned class, and banter the supposed subtilties and refinements of philosophy, are here heaped on the school of Socrates, and often delivered in a very comic manner. The worthy Strepsiades, whose home-bred understanding and mother-wit are quite overwhelmed with astonishment at the subtle tricks of the school-philosophers, until at last his own experience teaches him to form a different judgment, is from the beginning to the end of the piece a most amusing character. Notwithstanding all this, however, the piece cannot overcome the defect arising from the oblique views on which it is based, and the superficial manner in which the philosophy of Socrates is treated,—at least not in

---

* τὰ μετίωρα.

† The ἥττων or ἄδικος, and the κρείττων or δίκαιος λόγος. Aristophanes makes the former manner of speaking the representative of the assuming and arrogant youth, and the latter of the old respectable education, and personifies them both.

‡ See Aristoph. *Frogs*, 1491. *Birds*, 1555. Eupolis had given a more correct picture of Socrates, at least in regard to his outward appearance. Bergk *de rel. com. Atticæ*, p. 353.

§ That this chorus loses its special character towards the end of the piece, and even preaches reverence of the gods, is a point of resemblance between it and the choruses in the *Acharnians* and the *Wasps*, who at least act rather according to the *general character* of the Greek chorus, which was on the whole the same for tragedy and comedy, than according to the *particular part* which has been assigned to them.

the eyes of any one who is unable to surrender himself to the delusion under which Aristophanes appears to have laboured.

§ 6. The following year (Ol. 89, 2. B.C. 422) brought the *Wasps* of Aristophanes on the stage. The *Wasps* is so connected with the *Clouds*, that it is impossible to mistake a similarity of design in the development of certain thoughts in each. The *Clouds*, especially in its original form, was directed against the young Athenians, who, as wrangling tricksters, vexed the simple inoffensive citizens of Athens by bringing them against their will into the law-courts. The *Wasps* is aimed at the old Athenians, who took their seats day after day in great masses as judges, and being compensated for their loss of time by the judicial fees established by Pericles, gave themselves up entirely to the decision of the causes, which had become infinitely multiplied by the obligation on the allies to try their suits at Athens, and by the party spirit in the state itself: whereby these old people had acquired far too surly and snarling a spirit, to the great damage of the accused. There are two persons opposed to one another in this piece; the old *Philocleon*, who has given up the management of his affairs to his son, and devoted himself entirely to his office of judge (in consequence of which he pays the profoundest respect to Cleon, the patron of the popular courts); and his son *Bdelycleon*, who has a horror of Cleon and of the severity of the courts in general. It is very remarkable how entirely the course of the action between these two characters corresponds to that in the Clouds, so that we can hardly mistake the intention of Aristophanes to make one piece the counterpart of the other. The irony of fate, which the aged Strepsiades experiences, when that which had been the greatest object of his wishes, namely, to have his son thoroughly imbued with the rhetorical fluency of the Sophists, soon turns out to be the greatest misfortune to him,—is precisely the same with the irony of which the young Bdelycleon is the object in the Wasps; for, after having directed all his efforts towards curing his father of his mania for the profession of judge, and having actually succeeded in doing so, (partly by establishing a private dicasterion at home, and partly by recommending to him the charms of a fashionable luxurious life, such as the young Athenians of rank were attached to,) he soon bitterly repents of the metamorphosis which he has effected, since the old man, by a strange mixture of his old-fashioned rude manners with the luxury of the day, allows his dissoluteness to carry him much farther than Bdelycleon had either expected or desired.

The *Wasps* is undoubtedly one of the most perfect of the plays of Aristophanes.* We have already remarked upon the happy invention

* We cannot by any means accept A. W. von Schlegel's judgment, that this play is inferior to the other comedies of Aristophanes, and we entirely approve of the warm apology by Mr. Mitchell, in his edition of the *Wasps*, 1835, the object of which has unfortunately prevented the editor from giving the comedy in its full proportions.

of the masks of the chorus.* The same spirit of amusing novelty pervades the whole piece. The most farcical scene is the first between two dogs, which Bdelycleon sets on foot for the gratification of his father, and in which not only is the whole judicial system of the Athenians parodied in a ludicrous manner, but also a particular law-suit between the demagogue Cleon and the general Laches appears in a comic contrast, which must have forced a laugh from the gravest of the spectators.

§ 7. We have still a fifth comedy, the *Peace*, which is connected with the hitherto unbroken series; it is established by a didascalia, which has been recently brought to light, that it was produced at the great Dionysia in Ol. 89, 3. B. C. 421. Accordingly, this play made its appearance on the stage shortly before the *peace of Nicias*, which concluded the first part of the Peloponnesian war, and, as was then fully believed, was destined to put a final stop to this destructive contest among the Greek states.

The subject of the *Peace* is essentially the same as that of the Acharnians, except that, in the latter, peace is represented as the wish of an individual only, in the former as wished for by all. In the Acharnians, the chorus is opposed to peace; in the *Peace*, it is composed of countrymen of Attica, and all parts of Greece, who are full of a longing desire for peace. It must, however, be allowed, that in dramatic interest the Acharnians far excels the Peace, which is greatly wanting in the unity of a strong comic action. It must, no doubt, have been highly amusing to see how Trygæus ascends to heaven on the back of an entirely new sort of Pegasus,—a dung beetle,—and there, amidst all kinds of dangers, in spite of the rage of the dæmon of war, carries off the goddess Peace, with her fair companions, Harvesthome and Mayday: † but the sacrifice on account of the peace, and the preparations for the marriage of Trygæus with Harvesthome, are split up into a number of separate scenes, without any direct progress of the action, and without any great vigour of comic imagination. It is also too obvious, that Aristophanes endeavours to diminish the tediousness of these scenes by some of those loose jokes, which never failed to produce their effect on the common people of Athens; and it must be allowed, in general, that the poet often expresses better rules in respect to his rivals than he has observed in his own pieces. ‡

§ 8. There is now a gap of some years in the hitherto unbroken chain of Aristophanic comedies; but our loss is fully compensated by the *Birds*, which was brought out in Ol. 91, 2. B. C. 414. If the *Achar-*

---

* Chap. XXVII. § 5.
† So we venture to translate 'Οπώρα and Θεωρία.
‡ It should be added, that according to the old grammarians Eratosthenes and Crates, there were two plays by Aristophanes with this title, though there is no indication that the one which has come down to us is not that which appeared in the year 421.

nians is a specimen of the youthful vigour of Aristophanes, it appears in the *Birds* displayed in all its splendour; and with a style, in which a proud flight of imagination is united with the coarsest jocularity and most genial humour.

The *Birds* belongs to a period when the power and dominion of Athens had attained to an extent and splendour which can only be compared to the time about Ol. 81, 1. B.C. 456, before the military power of Athens was overthrown in Egypt. Athens had, by the very favourable peace of Nicias, strengthened her authority on the sea and in the coasts of Asia Minor; had shaken the policy of the Peloponnese by skilful intrigues; had brought her revenues to the highest point they ever attained; and finally had formed the plan of extending her authority by sea and on the coasts, over the western part of the Mediterranean, by the expedition to Sicily, which had commenced under the most favourable auspices. The disposition of the Athenians at this period is known to us from Thucydides: they allowed their demagogues and soothsayers to conjure up before them the most brilliant visionary prospects; henceforth nothing appeared unattainable; people gave themselves up, in general, to the intoxication of extravagant hopes. The hero of the day was Alcibiades, with his frivolity, his presumption, and that union of a calculating understanding with a bold, unfettered imagination, for which he was so distinguished; and even when he was lost to Athens by the unfortunate prosecution of the Hermocopidæ, the disposition which he had excited still survived for a considerable time.

It was at this time that Aristophanes composed his *Birds*. In order to comprehend this comedy in its connexion with the events of the day, and, on the other hand, not to attribute to it more than it really contains, it is especially necessary to take a rigorous and exact view of the action of the piece. Two Athenians, *Peisthetærus* and *Euelpides,* (whom we may call *Agitator* and *Hopegood,*) are sick and tired of the restless life at Athens, and the number of law-suits there, and have wandered out into the wide world in search of Hoopoo, an old mythological kinsman of the Athenians.* They soon find him in a rocky desert, where the whole host of birds assemble at the call of Hoopoo: for some time they are disposed to treat the two strangers of human race as national enemies; but are at last induced, on the recommendation of Hoopoo, to give them a hearing. Upon this, Agitator lays before them his grand ideas about the primeval sovereignty of the birds, the important rights and privileges they have lost, and how they ought to win them all back again by founding a great city for the whole race of birds: and this would remind the spectators of the plan of centralization, (συνοι-

---

* It is said to have been, in fact, the Thracian king Tereus, who had married Pandion's daughter Procne, and was turned into a hoopoo, his wife being metamorphosed into a nightingale.

κισμός,) which the Athenian statesmen of the day often employed for the
establishment of democracy, even in the Peloponnese. While Agitator
undertakes all the solemnities which belonged to the foundation of a
Greek city, and drives away the crowd, which is soon collected, of priests,
writers of hymns, prophets, land-surveyors, inspectors-general, and legis-
lators,—scenes full of satirical reflexion on the conduct of the Athenians
in their colonies and in allied states,—Hopegood superintends the building of this castle-in-the-air, this *Cloudcuckootown*, (Νεφελοκοκκυγία,) and
shortly after a messenger makes his appearance with a most amusing
description of the way in which the great fabric was constructed by the
labours of the different species of birds. Agitator treats this description
as a lie ;* and the spectators are also sensible that Cloudcuckootown
exists only in imagination, since Iris, the messenger of the gods, flies
past without having perceived, on her way from heaven to earth, the
faintest trace of the great blockading fortress. † The affair creates all
the more sensation among men on this account, and a number of swag-
gerers come to get their share in the promised distribution of wings,
without Agitator being able to make any use of those new citizens for
his city. As, however, men leave off sacrificing to the gods, and pay
honour to the birds only, the gods themselves are obliged to enter into
the imposture, and bear a part in the absurdities which result from it.
An agreement is made in which Zeus himself gives up his sovereignty to
Agitator ; this is brought about by a contrivance of Agitator ; he has the
skill to win over Hercules, who has come as an ambassador from the
gods, with the savoury smell of certain birds, whom he has arrested as
aristocrats, and is roasting for his dinner. At the end of the comedy
Agitator appears with Sovereignty, (Βασίλεια,) splendidly attired as
his bride, brandishing the thunder-bolts of Zeus, and in a triumphal
hymeneal procession, accompanied by the whole tribe of birds.

In this short sketch we have purposely omitted all the subordinate
parts, amusing and brilliant as they are, in order to make sure of obtaining a correct view of the whole piece. People have often overlooked
the general scope of the play, and have sought for a signification in
the details, which the plan of the whole would not allow. It is impossible that Athens can have been intended under Cloudcuckootown, especially as this city of the birds is treated as a mere imagination : moreover,
the birds are real birds throughout the play, and if Aristophanes had
intended to represent his countrymen under these masks, the characteristics of the Athenians would have been shown in them in a very different

* v. 1167. ἴσα γὰρ ἀληθῶς φαίνεταί μοι ψεύδεσιν.
† Of course we see nothing of the new city on the stage, which throughout the
piece represents a rocky place with trees about it, and with the house of the Epops
in the centre, which at the end of the play is converted into the kitchen where the
birds are roasted.

Political Philosophy.

The following are some of the Subjects to be treated of in this Series:—

I. THE GENERAL PRINCIPLES OF THE SOCIAL UNION, AND OF GOVERNMENT.

Origin of the Social Compact.

The application of the Doctrine of Expediency to the Formation of Governments, to changes of Government, and to the Right of Property.

The Doctrine of Resistance, and its limits in Theory and Practice, and the Parties in this Country to which it has given rise.

The Supreme Power in all States, in its three Branches—Executive, Legislative, and Judicial.

The Division of Governments into Monarchical, Aristocratical, and Democratical.

II. MONARCHICAL GOVERNMENT.

The General Principles of Monarchy, and its division into Despotic or Absolute, and Limited or Constitutional, and into Elective and Hereditary.

Eastern Despotisms.

The Russian Government.

The Feudal System.

The Principles of Constitutional Monarchy.

European Governments.

III. ARISTOCRATIC GOVERNMENT.

Its Principles, and their Modification.

The Disadvantages of this form of Polity.

The Constitution and History of Certain Aristocratic Governments.

The Mixture of Aristocracy in other Governments, and its influence.

The deduction of Aristocracy from the Feudal System.

IV. DEMOCRATIC GOVERNMENT.

The Nature of the Democratic Principle—its Advantages and Disadvantages.

V. MIXED MONARCHY.

The advantages of studying our own Constitution minutely, and comparing its Structure and Formation with those of Foreign Countries, as Physiologists study Comparative Anatomy

The source from which the true knowledge of our Constitution can be drawn,—Law and History, especially Parliamentary History.

The Principles on which, theoretically and practically, the different Checks in the Constitution act, and the rise and progress of those Checks previous to the Commonwealth.

The Commonwealth—Pym, Hampden, Falkland, Cromwell. Its Effects on Liberty.

The Causes which led to the Restoration.—Monk, Clarendon.

The Revolution of 1688.—King William, Lord Somers.

The Nature in detail of our Constitutional Checks, their practical action, and the errors of speculative men on this subject.

The Use and Abuse of Party.

The Checks on the Supreme Legislative Power in the various action of public opinion, comprehending the Use and Abuse of Associations, Meetings, and the Press.

The Structure of the French, Spanish, and Portuguese Governments, and those of the New States of South America.

VI. THE FUNCTIONS OF GOVERNMENT—Its Structure having now been examined.*

The Judicial System, both preparatory and final, or Police and Judicature, in its General Principles.

The Military System, in its General Principles, both as relates to defence, economy, and civil policy.

The Military Policy of the European Powers.

The Military System as connected with Foreign Policy—the Principles of that Policy, and the use and abuse of the Doctrine of the Balance of Powers.

The Financial System in its General Principles, and under its two great divisions of Taxation and the Funding System.

The Financial System of Foreign Countries, particularly Spain, Germany, Holland, France, and America.

The Financial System of England.

VII. POLITICAL ECONOMY.

The Grounds upon which the Government may in some cases advantageously interfere with the proper pursuits of the people, like Judicature, Revenue, and Defence.

Public Works and Joint Stock Companies—Hospitals.

Public Protection, and the principles which should guide it.

Religious Establishments, and their principal advantages and disadvantages.

The Currency, or Public Coin and Paper Money, and the principles which govern it, with the History of the Circulation.

The interference of Government where men should be left to themselves, and the origin and evils of the mercantile system.

Monopolies and other institutions growing out of the mercantile system.

Interference with the Progress of Population, and the principle of population generally.

The influence of the Progress of Population upon the condition of the Labouring Classes, and the principles thence derived respecting Provisions for the Poor.

The History of provisions respecting Mendicity and the Poor in this and other countries.

The interference of Government with Capital in the Plantation of Colonies ; and the principles of Colonial Policy, including the use and abuse of Colonial Establishments.

French Economists, Quesnai, Mirabeau, Turgot—Scotch school, Smith and Hume—English school, Ricardo and Malthus.

* The Sixth Head ought to be ranked with the Seventh, except that the line is conveniently drawn between the necessary and unnecessary interference of Government.

LONDON: Printed by WILLIAM CLOWES and SONS, Stamford Street.

LIBRARY OF USEFUL KNOWLEDGE.

HISTORY OF THE
LITERATURE OF GREECE.
VOL. II.—PART II.

COMMITTEE.

Chairman—The Right Hon. LORD BROUGHAM, F.R.S., Member of the
National Institute of France.
Vice Chairman—JOHN WOOD, Esq.
Treasurer—WILLIAM TOOKE, Esq., F.R.S.

ALFRED AINGER, Esq.
WM. ALLEN, Esq., F.R. and R.A.S.
CHARLES ANSELL, Esq.
CAPTAIN BEAUFORT, R.N. F.R. and R.A.S.
GEORGE BIRKBECK, M.D.
GEORGE BURROWS, M.D.
PETER STAFFORD CAREY, Esq., A.M.
JOHN CONOLLY, M.D.
WILLIAM COULSON, Esq.
R. DAVIS CRAIG, Esq.
J. F. DAVIS, Esq., F.R.S.
H. T. DE LA BECHE, Esq., F.R.S.
THE RIGHT HON. LORD DENMAN.
SAMUEL DUCKWORTH, Esq.
THE RIGHT REV. THE BISHOP OF DURHAM, D.D.
SIR HY. ELLIS, Prin. Lib. Brit. Mus.
T. F. ELLIS, Esq., A.M., F.R.A.S.
JOHN ELLIOTSON, M.D., F.R.S.
GEORGE EVANS, Esq., M.P.
THOMAS FALCONER, Esq.
I. L. GOLDSMID, Esq., F.R. and R.A.S.
FRANCIS HENRY GOLDSMID, Esq.
B. GOMPERTZ, Esq., F.R. and R.A.S.
J. T. GRAVES, Esq., A.M., F.R.S.
G. B. GREENOUGH, Esq., F.R. and L.S.
M. D. HILL, Esq., Q.C.
ROWLAND HILL, Esq., F.R.A.S.
RIGHT HON. SIR J. C. HOBHOUSE, Bart., M.P.
THOMAS HODGKIN, M.D.
DAVID JARDINE, Esq., A.M.

HENRY B. KER, Esq.
THOMAS HEWITT KEY, Esq., A.M.
SIR CHARLES LEMON, Bart., M.P.
GEORGE C. LEWIS, Esq., A.M.
THOMAS HENRY LISTER, Esq.
JAMES LOCH, Esq., M.P., F.G.S.
GEORGE LONG, Esq., A.M.
HY. MALDEN, Esq, A.M.
ARTHUR T. MALKIN, Esq., A.M.
MR. SERJEANT MANNING.
R. I. MURCHISON, Esq., F.R.S., F.G.S.
THE RIGHT HON. LORD NUGENT.
W. SMITH O'BRIEN, Esq., M.P.
THE RIGHT HON. SIR HY. PARNELL, Bart., M.P.
RICHARD QUAIN, Esq.
P. M. ROGET, M.D., Sec. R.S., F.R.A.S.
EDWARD ROMILLY, Esq., A.M.
R. W. ROTHMAN, Esq., A.M.
SIR MARTIN A. SHEE, P.R.A., F.R.S.
THE RIGHT HON. EARL SPENCER.
SIR GEO. T. STAUNTON, Bart., M.P.
JOHN TAYLOR, Esq., F.R.S.
A. T. THOMSON, M.D.
THOMAS VARDON, Esq.
JAMES WALKER, Esq., F.R.S.
HY. WAYMOUTH, Esq.
THOS. WEBSTER, Esq., A.M.
J. WHISHAW, Esq., A.M. F.R.S.
THE HON. JOHN WROTTESLEY, A.M., F.R.A.S.
JOHN ASHTON YATES, Esq., M.P.

THOMAS COATES, Esq., *Secretary*, 59, Lincoln's Inn Fields.

LONDON:
PUBLISHED BY THE SOCIETY FOR THE DIFFUSION OF
USEFUL KNOWLEDGE,

59, LINCOLN'S INN FIELDS.

No. 331.] *September* 1, 1840. [*Price Sixpence.*

POLITICAL SERIES.

The Numbers appear on the 15th of every Month.

A General MAP of RUSSIA IN EUROPE, price 6*d.*, has just been published by the Society, which has also issued a more detailed Map, in Eight Parts, price 6*d.* each.

LIBRARY OF USEFUL KNOWLEDGE.

The following Works are in course of Publication at the Office of the Society:—

I.

THE GEOGRAPHY OF AMERICA.

II.

THE HISTORY OF GREEK LITERATURE, Vol. II.

way.* Besides, it is very difficult to believe that Agitator and Hopegood were intended to represent any Athenian statesmen in particular; the chief rulers of the people at that time could not possibly have shown themselves diametrically opposed, as Agitator does, to the judicial and legislative system, and to the sycophancy of the Athenians. But according to the poet's express declaration, they are Athenians, the genuine offspring of Athens, and it is clear, that in these two characters, he intended to give two perfect specimens of the Athenians of the day; the one is an intriguing projector, a restless, inventive genius, who knows how to give a plausible appearance to the most irrational schemes; the other is an honest, credulous fool, who enters into the follies of his companion with the utmost simplicity.† Consequently, the whole piece is a satire on Athenian frivolity and credulity, on that building of castles in the air, and that dreaming expectation of a life of luxury and ease to which the Athenian people gave themselves up in the mass: but the satire is so general, there is so little of anger and bitterness, so much of fantastic humour in it, that no comedy could make a more agreeable and harmless impression. We must, in this, dissent entirely from the opinion of the Athenian judges, who, though they crowned the *Knights*, awarded only the second prize to the *Birds*; it seems that they were better able to appreciate the force of a violent personal attack than the creative fulness of comic originality.

§ 9. We have two plays of Aristophanes which came out in Ol. 92, 1; B. C. 411, (if our chronological data are correct,) the *Lysistrata* and the *Thesmophoriazusæ*. A didascalia, which has come down to us, assigns the *Lysistrata* to this year, in which, after the unfortunate issue of the Sicilian expedition, the occupation of Deceleia by the Spartans, and their subsidiary treaty with the king of Persia, the war began to press heavily upon the Athenians. At the same time the constitution of Athens had fallen into a fluctuating state, which ended in an oligarchy: a board of commissioners, (πρόβουλοι,) consisting of men of the greatest rank and consideration, superintended all the affairs of state; and, a few months after the representation of the Thesmophoriazusæ, began the rule of the Four hundred. Aristophanes, who had all along been attached to the peace-party, which consisted of the thriving landed proprietors, now gave himself up entirely to his longing for peace, as if all civic rule and harmony in the state must necessarily be restored by a cessation from war. In the Lysistrata this longing for peace is exhibited in a farcical form, which is almost without a parallel for extravagant indecency; the

* That several points applicable to Athens occur in the Cloudcookootown (the Acropolis, with the worship of Minerva Polias, the Pelasgian wall, &c.) proves nothing but this, that the Athenians, who plan the city, made use of names common at home, as was always the custom in colonies.

† We may remark that Euelpides only remains on the stage till the plan of Nephelococcygia is formed: after that, the poet has no further employment for him.

women are represented as compelling their husbands to come to terms,
by refusing them the exercise of their marital rights; but the care with
which he abstains from any direct political satire shows how fluctuating
all relations were at that time, and how little Aristophanes could tell
whither to turn himself with the vigour of a man who has chosen his
party.

In the *Thesmophoriazusæ*, nearly contemporary with the Lysistrata,*
Aristophanes keeps still further aloof from politics, and plunges into
literary criticism, (such as before only served him for a collateral ornament,) which he helps out with a complete apparatus of indecent jokes.
Euripides passed for a woman-hater at Athens: but without any
reason; for, in his tragedies, the charming, susceptible mind of woman
is as often the motive of good as of bad actions.   General opinion, however, had stamped him as a misogynist.   Accordingly, the piece turns
on the fiction that the women had resolved at the feast of the Thesmo-
phoria, when they were quite alone, to take vengeance on Euripides, and
punish him with death; and that Euripides was desirous of getting
some one whom he might pass off for a woman, and send as such into
this assembly.   The first person who occurs to his mind, the delicate,
effeminate Agathon—an excellent opportunity for travestying Agathon's
manner—will not undertake the business, and only furnishes the costume,
in which the aged Mnesilochus, the father-in-law and friend of Euripides,
is dressed up as a woman.   Mnesilochus conducts his friend's cause
with great vigour; but he is denounced, his sex is discovered, and, on
the complaint of the women, he is committed to the custody of a Scythian
police-slave, until Euripides, having in vain endeavoured, in the guise of
a tragic Menelaus and Perseus, to carry off this new Helen and Andromeda, entices the Scythian from his watch over Mnesilochus by an
artifice of a grosser and more material kind.   The chief joke in the
whole piece is that Aristophanes, though he pretends to punish Euripides for his calumnies against women, is much more severe upon the
fair sex than Euripides had ever been.

* The date assigned to the *Thesmophoriazusæ*, Ol. 92, 1. B.C. 411, rests partly on
its relation to the *Andromeda* of Euripides, (see chap. XXV. § 17, note,) which
was a year older, and which, from its relation to the *Frogs*, (*Schol. Aristoph. Frogs*,
53,) is placed in Ol. 91. 4—B. C. 412.   No doubt the expression ὀγδόῳ ἔτει would
also allow us to place the Andromeda in 413; and therefore, the Thesmophoriazusæ
in 412; but this is opposed by the clear mention of the defeat of Charminus in a
sea-fight, (*Thesmoph.* 804;) which falls, according to Thucyd. viii. 41, in the very
beginning of 411.   Without setting aside the *Schol. Frogs*, 53, and some other
corresponding notices in the Ravenna scholia on the Thesmophoriazusæ, we cannot
bring down this comedy to the year 410: consequently, the passage in v. 808 about
the deposed councillors, cannot refer to the expulsion of the Five hundred by the
oligarchy of the Four hundred, (Thucyd. viii. 69,) which did not take place till
after the Dionysia of the year 411; but to the circumstance that the βουλευταί of the
year 412, Ol. 91, 4, were obliged to give up a considerable part of their functions
to the board of πρόβουλοι, (Thucyd. viii. 1.)

§ 10. The literary criticism, which seems to have been the principal employment of Aristophanes during the last gloomy years of the Peloponnesian war, came out in its most perfect form in the *Frogs*, which was acted Ol. 93, 3. B. C. 405, and is one of the most masterly productions which the muse of comedy has ever conceded to her favourites. The idea, on which the whole is built, is beautiful and grand. Dionysus, the god of the Attic stage, here represented as a young Athenian fop, who gives himself out as a connoisseur of tragedies, is much distressed at the great deficiency of tragic poets after the deaths of Euripides and Sophocles, and is resolved to go and bring up a tragedian from the other world,—if possible, Euripides.* He gets Charon to ferry him over the pool which forms the boundary of the infernal regions, (where he is obliged to pull himself to the merry croaking of the marsh frogs,)† and arrives, after various dangers, at the place where the chorus of the happy souls who have been initiated into the mysteries (*i. e.* those who are capable of enjoying properly the freedom and merriment of comedy) perform their songs and dances: he and his servant Xanthias have, however, still many amusing adventures to undergo at Pluto's gate before they are admitted. It so happens that a strife has arisen in the subterranean world between Æschylus, who had hitherto occupied the tragic throne, and the newly arrived Euripides, who lays claim to it: and Dionysus connects this with his own plan by promising to take with him to the upper regions whichever of the two gains the victory in this contest. The contest which ensues is a peculiar mixture of jest and earnest: it extends over every department of tragic act,—the subject-matter and moral effects, the style and execution, prologues, choral songs, and monodies, and often, though in a very comic manner, hits the right point. The comedian, however, does not hesitate to support, rather by bold figures than by proofs, his opinion that Æschylus had uttered profound observations, sterling truths, full of moral significance; while Euripides, with his subtle reasonings, rendered insecure the basis of religious faith and moral principles on which the weal of the state rested. Thus, at the end of the play, the two tragedians proceed to weigh their verses; and the powerful sayings of Æschylus make the pointed thoughts of Euripides kick the beam. In his fundamental opinion about the relative merits of these poets, Aristophanes is undoubtedly so far right, that the immediate feeling for and natural consciousness of the right and the good which breathes in the works of Æschylus, was far more conducive to the moral strength of mind and public virtue

---

* He is chiefly desirous of seeing the Andromeda of Euripides, which was exceedingly popular with the people of Abdera also. Lucian. *Quom. conscr. sit Hist.* 1.

† The part of the *Frogs* was indeed performed by the chorus, but they were not seen, (*i. e.* it was a *parachoregema*;) probably the choreutæ were placed in the *hyposcenium*, (a space under the stage,) and therefore on the same elevation as the orchestra.

of his fellow citizens than a mode of reasoning like that in Euripides, which brings all things before its tribunal, and, as it were, makes everything dependent on the doubtful issue of a trial.   But Aristophanes is wrong in reproaching Euripides personally with a tendency which exercised such an irresistible influence on his age in general.   If it was the aim of the comedian to bring back the Athenian public to that point of literary taste when Æschylus was fully sufficient for them, it would have been necessary for him to be able to lock the wheels of time, and to screw back the machinery which propelled the mind in its forward progress.

We should not omit to mention the political references which occasionally appear by the side of the literary contents of this comedy. Aristophanes maintains his position of opponent to the violent democrats: he attacks the demagogue Cleophon, then in the height of his power: in the parabasis he recommends the people, covertly but significantly enough, to make peace with and be reconciled to the persecuted oligarchs, who had ruled over Athens during the time of the Four hundred; recognizing, however, the inability of the people to save themselves from the ruin which threatens them by their own power and prudence, he hints that they should submit to the mighty genius of Alcibiades, though he was certainly no old Athenian according to the ideal of Aristophanes: this suggestion is contained in two remarkable verses, which he puts into the mouth of Æschylus :—

> " 'Twere best to rear no lion in the state,
>   But when 'tis done, his will must not be thwarted ;"—

a piece of advice which would have been more in season had it been delivered ten years earlier.

§ 11. Aristophanes is the only one of the great Athenian poets who survived the Peloponnesian war, in the course of which Sophocles and Euripides, Cratinus and Eupolis, had all died.   We find him still writing for the stage for a series of years after the close of the war.   His *Ecclesiazusæ* was probably brought out in Ol. 96, 4. B. C. 392: it is a piece of wild drollery, but based upon the same political creed which Aristophanes had professed for thirty years.   Democracy had been restored in its worst features; the public money was again expended for private purposes; the demagogue Agyrrhius was catering for the people by furnishing them with pay for their attendance in the public assembly; and the populace were following to-day one leader, and to-morrow another.   In this state of affairs, according to the fiction of Aristophanes, the women resolve to take upon themselves the whole management of the city, and carry their point by appearing in the assembly in men's clothes, principally " because this was the only thing that had not yet been attempted at Athens ;"* and

---

* *Ecclesiaz.* v. 456. Ἰδέκει γὰρ τοῦτο μόνον ἐν τῇ πόλει
  οὔπω γιγνῆσθαι.

people hoped that, according to an old oracle, the wildest resolution which they made would turn out to their benefit. The women then establish an excellent Utopia, in which property and wives are to be in common, and the interests of the ugly of both sexes are specially provided for, a conception which is followed out into all its absurd consequences with a liberal mixture of humour and indecency.

From this combination of a serious thought, by way of foundation, with the boldest creations of a riotous imagination, the Ecclesiazusæ must be classed with the works which appeared during the vigour of Attic comedy: but the technical arrangement shows, in a manner which cannot be mistaken, the poverty and thriftiness of the state at this time.* The chorus is obviously fitted out very parsimoniously; its masks were easily made, as they represented only Athenian women, who at first appear with beards and men's cloaks; besides, it required but little practice, as it had but little to sing. The whole parabasis is omitted, and its place is supplied by a short address, in which the chorus, before it leaves the stage, calls upon the judges to decide fairly and impartially.

These outward deviations from the original plan of the old comedy are in the *Plutus* combined with great alterations in the internal structure; and thus furnish a plain transition to the *middle comedy*, as it is called. The extant Plutus is not that which the poet produced in Ol. 92, 4. B.C. 408, but that which came out twenty years later in Ol. 97, 4. B.C. 388, and was the last piece which the aged poet brought forward himself; for two plays which he composed subsequently, the *Cocalus* and *Æolosicon*, were brought out by his son Araros. In the extant Plutus, Aristophanes tears himself away altogether from the great political interests of the state. His satire in this piece is, in part, universally applicable to all races and ages of men, for it is directed against defects and perversities which attach themselves to our every-day life; and, in part, it is altogether personal, as it attacks individuals selected from the mass at the caprice of the poet, in order that the jokes may take a deeper and wider root. The conception on which it is based is of lasting significance: the god of riches has, in his blindness, fallen into the hands of the worst of men, and has himself suffered greatly thereby: a worthy, respectable citizen, *Chremylus*, provides for the recovery of his sight, and so makes many good people prosperous, and reduces many knaves to poverty. From the more general nature of the fable it follows that the persons also have the general character of their condition and employments, in which the piece approximates to the manner of the middle comedy, as it also does in the more decent, less

---

* The choregiæ were not discontinued, but people endeavoured to make them less expensive every year. See Boeckh, *Public Economy of Athens*, book iii. § 22.

offensive, but at the same time less genial nature of the language. The alteration, however, does not run through the play so as to bring the new species of comedy before us in its complete form; here and there we feel the breath of the old comedy around us, and we cannot avoid the melancholy conviction that the genial comedian has survived the best days of his art, and has therefore become insecure and unequal in his application of it.

CHAPTER XXIX.

§ 1. Characteristics of Cratinus. § 2. Eupolis. § 3. Peculiar tendencies of Crates; his connexion with Sicilian comedy. § 4. Sicilian comedy originates in the Doric farces of Megara. § 5. Events in the life of Epicharmus; general tendency and nature of his comedy. § 6. The middle Attic comedy.; poets of this class akin to those of the Sicilian comedy in many of their pieces. § 7. Poets of the new comedy the immediate successors of those of the middle comedy. How the new comedy becomes naturalized at Rome. § 8. Public morality at Athens at the time of the new comedy. § 9. Character of the new comedy in connexion therewith.

§ 1. CRATINUS and Eupolis, Pherecrates and Hermippus, Telecleides and Plato, and several of those who competed with them for the prize of comedy, are known to us from the names of a number of their pieces which have come down to our time; and also from the short quotations from their plays by subsequent authors; these furnish us with abundant materials for an inquiry into the details of Athenian life, public and private, but are of little use for a description like the present, which is based on the contents of individual works and on the characteristics of the different poets.

Of *Cratinus*, in particular, we learn more from the short but pregnant notices of him by Aristophanes, than from the very mutilated fragments of his works. It is clear that he was well fitted by nature for the wild and merry dances of the Bacchic Comus. The spirit of comedy spoke out as clearly and as powerfully in him as that of tragedy did in Æschylus. He gave himself up with all the might of his genius to the fantastic humour of this amusement; and the scattered sparks of his wit proceeded from a soul imbued with the magnanimous honesty of the older Athenians. His personal attacks were free from all fear or regard to the consequences. As opposed to Cratinus, Aristophanes appeared as a well educated man, skilled and apt in speech, and not untinged with that very sophistic training of Euripides, against which he so systematically inveighed; and thus we find it asked in a fragment of Cratinus :—"Who art thou, thou hair-splitting orator ; thou hunter after sentences ; thou petty Euripidaristophanes ?" *

Even the names of his choruses show, to a certain extent, on what various and bold devices the poems of Cratinus were based. He not only made up a chorus of mere Archilochuses and Cleobulines, *i. e.* of abusive slanderers. and gossiping women ; he also brought on a number of Ulysseses and Chirons as a chorus, and even Panopteses, *i. e.* beings like the Argos-Panoptes of mythology, who had heads turned both ways with innumerable eyes,† by which, according to an ingenious explanation, ‡ he intended to represent the scholars of Hippo, a speculative philosopher of the day, whose followers pretended that nothing in heaven or earth remained concealed from them. Even the riches (πλοῦτοι) and the laws (νόμοι) of Athens formed choruses in the plays of Cratinus, as, in general, Attic comedy took the liberty of personifying whatever it pleased.

The play of Cratinus, with the plot of which we are best acquainted, is the *Pytine*, or "bottle," which he wrote in the last year of his life. In his later years Cratinus was undoubtedly much given to drinking, and Aristophanes and the other comedians were already sneering at him as a doting old man, whose poetry was fuddled with wine. Upon this the old comedian suddenly roused himself, and with such vigour and success that he won the prize, in Ol. 89, 1. B.C. 423, from all his rivals, including Aristophanes, who brought out the "Clouds" on the occasion. The piece which Cratinus thus produced was the *Pytine*. With magnanimous candour the poet made himself the subject of his own comedy. The comic muse was represented as the lawful wife of Cratinus, as the faithful partner of his younger days, and she complained bitterly of the neglect with which she was then treated in consequence of her husband having become attached to another lady, the bottle. She goes to the Archons, and brings a plaint of criminal neglect (κάκωσις) against him ; if her husband will not return to her she is to obtain a divorce from him. The consequence is, that the poet returns to his senses, and his old love is re-awakened in his bosom ; and at the end he raises himself up in all the power and beauty of his poetical genius, and goes so far in the drama that his friends try to stop his mouth, lest he should carry away everything with the overflowing of his imagery and versification. § In this piece, Cratinus did not merit the reproach which has been generally cast upon him, that he could not work out his own excellent conceptions, but, as it were, destroyed them himself.

* Τίς δὲ σύ ; (κομψός τις ἴρωτε διατής)
'Υπολιπτολόγος, γνωμιδιώτης, εὐριπιδαριστοφανίζων·
The answer of Aristophanes is mentioned above, Chap. XXV., § 7.
† Κράνια δισσὰ φερεῖν, ὀφθαλμοὶ δ' οὐκ ἀριθμητοί·
‡ Bergk *de reliquiis Comediæ Atticæ antiquæ*, p. 162.
§ *Cratini fragmenta coll. Runkel*, p. 50. Meineke, *Hist. Crit. Com. Græc.*, vol. I. p. 54, vol. II. p. 116—132.

So early as the time when Cratinus was in his prime, (Ol. 85, 1. B.C. 440,) a law was passed limiting the freedom of comic satire. It is very probable that it was under the constraint of this law, (which, however, was not long in force,) that the Ulysseses ('Οδυσσεῖς) of Cratinus was brought out; a piece of which it was remarked by the old literary critics,* that it came nearer to the character of the middle comedy: it probably abstained from all personal, and especially from political satire, and kept itself within the circle of the general relations of mankind, in which it was easy for the poet to avail himself of the old mythical story,—Ulysses in the cave of Polyphemus.

§ 2. A Roman poet, who was very careful in his choice of words, and who is remarkable for a certain pregnancy of expression,† calls Cratinus "the bold," and in the same passage opposes EUPOLIS to him, as "the angry." Although Eupolis is stated to have been celebrated for his elegance, and for the aptness of his witticisms, as well as for his imaginative powers,‡ his style was probably marked by a strong hatred of the prevailing depravity, and by much bitterness of satire. He himself claimed a share in the "Knights" of Aristophanes, in which personal satire prevails more than in any other comedy of that poet. On the other hand, Aristophanes maintains that Eupolis, in his *Maricas*, had imitated the "Knights," and spoiled it by injudicious additions.§ Of the *Maricas*, which was produced Ol. 89, 3. B.C. 421, we only know thus much, that under this slave's name he exhibited the demagogue Hyperbolus, who succeeded to Cleon's place in the favour of the people, and who was, like Cleon, represented as a low-minded, ill-educated fellow; the worthy Nicias was introduced in the piece chiefly as the butt of his tricks. The most virulent, however, of the plays of Eupolis was probably the *Baptæ*, which is often mentioned by old writers, but in such terms that it is not easy to gather a clear notion of this very singular drama. The view which appears most probable to the author of these pages is, that the comedy of Eupolis was directed against the club (ἑταιρία) of Alcibiades, and especially against a sort of mixture of profligacy, which despised the conventional morality of the day, and frivolity, and which set at nought the old religion of Athens, and thus naturally assumed the garb of mystic and foreign religions. In this piece Alcibiades and his comrades appeared

---

* *Platonius de Comœdia*, p. viii. That the piece contained a caricature (διασυρμόν τινα) of Homer's Odyssey is not to be understood as if Cratinus had wished to ridicule Homer.

            † Audaci quicunque adflate Cratino,
            Iratum Eupolidem prægrandi cum sene palles.
Persius, I. 124. The *Vita Aristophanis* agrees with this.

‡ φαντασία, εὐφάντακτος. Platonius also speaks highly of the energy (ἐνψηλός) and grace (ἐπίχαρις) of Eupolis. He perhaps exaggerates the latter quality. See Meineke, *Hist. Crit. Com. Gr.* vol. I. p. 107.

§ Aristophanes, *Clouds*, 553.

under the name of *Baptæ*, (which seems to have been borrowed from a mystic rite of baptism which they practised,) as worshippers of a barbarian deity Cotys or Cotytto, whose wild worship was celebrated with the din of loud music, and was made a cloak for all sorts of debauchery; and the picture given of these rites in the piece, if we may judge from what Juvenal says,* must have been very powerful and impressive.

Eupolis composed two plays which obviously had some connexion with one another, and which represented the political condition of Athens at the time; the one in its domestic, the other in its external relations. In the former, which was called the *Demi*, the boroughs of Attica, of which the whole people consisted, (οἱ δῆμοι,) formed the persons of the chorus; and Myronides, a distinguished general and statesman of the time of Pericles, who had survived the great men of his own day, and now in extreme old age felt that he stood alone in the midst of a degenerate race, was represented as descending to the other world to restore to Athens one of her old leaders; and he does in fact bring back Solon, Miltiades, and Pericles.† The poet contrived, no doubt, to construct a very agreeable plot by a portraiture of these men, in which respect for the greatness of their characters was combined with many merry jests, and by exhibiting, on the other side, in the most energetic manner, the existing state of Athens, destitute as she then was of good statesmen and generals. From some fragments it appears that the old heroes felt very uncomfortable in this upper world of ours, and that the chorus had to intreat them most earnestly not to give up the state-affairs and the army of Athens to a set of effeminate and presumptuous young men: at the conclusion of the piece, the chorus offers up to the spirits of the heroes, with all proper ceremonies, the wool-bound olive boughs, (εἰρεσιῶναι,) by which, according to the religious rites of the Greeks, it had supported its supplications to them, and so honours them as gods. In the *Poleis*, the chorus consisted of the allied or rather tributary cities; the island of Chios, which had always remained true to Athens, and was therefore better treated than the others, stood advantageously prominent among them, and Cyzicus in the Propontis brought up the rear. Beyond this little is known about the connexion of the plot.

§ 3. Among the remaining comic poets of this time, CRATES stands most prominently forward, because he differs most from the others. From being an actor in Cratinus' plays, Crates had risen to the rank of

---

* Juvenal, II. 91.

† That Myronides brings up Pericles is clear from a comparison of Plutarch, *Pericl.* 24, with the passages of Aristides, Platonius, and others, (Raspe *de Eupolid. Δήμοις et Πόλισιν. Lips.* 1832.) Pericles asks Myronides, " Why he brings him back to life? are there no good people in Athens? if his son by Aspasia is not a great statesman?" and so forth. From this it is clear that it was Myronides who had conveyed him from the other world.

a comic poet; he was, however, any thing but an imitator of his master. On the contrary, he entirely gave up the field which Cratinus and the other comedians had chosen as their regular arena, namely, political satire; perhaps because in his inferior position he lacked the courage to attack from the stage the most powerful demagogues, or because he thought that department already exhausted of its best materials. His skill lay in the more artificial design and developement of his plots,* and the interest of his pieces depended on the connexion of the stories which they involved. Accordingly, Aristophanes says of him,† that he had feasted the Athenians at a trifling expense, and had with great sobriety given them the enjoyment of his most ingenious inventions. Crates is said to have been the first who introduced the drunkard on the stage; and *Pherecrates*, who of the later Attic comedians most resembled Crates,‡ painted the glutton with most colossal features.

§ 4. Aristotle connects Crates with the Sicilian comic poet EPICHAR-MUS, and no doubt he stood in a nearer relation to him than the other comedians of Athens. This will be the right place to speak of this celebrated poet, as it would have disturbed the historic developement of the Attic drama had we turned our attention at an earlier period to the comedy of Sicily. As we have already remarked, (chap.XXVII. § 3,) Sicilian comedy is connected with the old farces of Megara, but took a different direction, and one quite peculiar to itself. The Megarian farces themselves did not exhibit the political character which was so early assumed by Attic comedy; but they cultivated a department of raillery which was unknown to the comedy of Aristophanes, that is, a ludicrous imitation of certain classes and conditions of common life. A lively and cheerful observation of the habits and manners connected with certain offices and professions soon enabled the comedian to observe something characteristic in them, and often something narrow-minded and partial, something quite foreign to the results of a liberal education, something which rendered the person awkward and unfitted for other employments, and so opened a wide field for satire and witticisms. In this way *Mæson*, an old Megarian comic actor and poet,§ constantly employed the mask of a cook or a scullion; consequently such persons were called Mæsones (μαίσωνες) at Athens,

---

* Aristot. *Poet.* c. 5. Τῶν δὲ Ἀθήνησι Κράτης πρῶτος ἦρξεν, ἀφέμενος τῆς ἰαμβικῆς ἰδέας, καθόλου λόγους ἢ μύθους ποιεῖν· i. e. "Of the Athenian comedians, Crates was the first who gave up personal satire, and began to make narratives or poems on more general subjects."

† *Knights*, 535. Comp. Meineke, *Hist. Crit. Com. Græc.*, p. 60.

‡ *Anonym. de Comœdia*, p. xxix.

§ There can be no doubt that he lived at a time when there existed by the side of the Attic comedy a Megarian drama of the same kind, of which Ecphantides, a predecessor of Cratinus, and other poets of the old comedy, spoke as a rough farcical entertainment. The Megarian comedian *Solymus* belongs to the same period.

and their jokes Mæsonian (μαισωνικά.)* A considerable element in such representations would consist of mimicry and absurd gestures, such as the Dorians seem to have been generallly more fond of than the Athenians ; the amusement furnished by the Spartan *Deicelictæ* (δεικήλικται) was made up of the imitation of certain characters taken from common life ; for instance, the character of a foreign physician represented in a sort of pantomime dance, and with the vulgar language of the lower orders.† The more probable supposition is, that this sort of comedy passed over to Sicily through the Doric colonies, as it is on the western boundaries of the Grecian world that we find a general prevalence of comic dramas in which the amusement consists in a recurrence of the same character and the same species of masks. The Oscan pastime of the *Atellanæ,* which went from Campania to Rome, was also properly designated by these standing characters ; and great as the distance was from the Dorians of the Peloponnese to the Oscans of Atella, we may nevertheless discern in the character-masks of the latter some clear traces of Greek influence.‡

In Sicily, comedy made its first appearance at Selinus, a Megarian colony. *Aristoxenus,* who composed comedies in the Dorian dialect, lived here before Epicharmus ; how long before him cannot be satisfactorily ascertained. In fact we know very little about him ; still it is remarkable that among the few records of him which we possess there is a verse which was the commencement of a somewhat long invective against soothsayers ;§ whence it is clear that he, too, occupied himself with the follies and absurdities of whole classes and conditions of men.

§ 5. The flourishing period of Sicilian comedy was that in which *Phormis, Epicharmus,* and *Deinolochus,* (the son or scholar of the latter,) wrote for the stage. Phormis is mentioned as the friend of Gelo and the instructor of his children. According to credible authorities, Epicharmus was a native of Cos, who went to Sicily with Cadmus, the tyrant of Cos, when he resigned his power and emigrated to that island, about Ol. 73, B.C. 488. Epicharmus at first resided a short time at the Sicilian Megara, where he probably first commenced his career as a comedian. Megara was conquered by Gelo, (Ol. 74, 1. or 2. B.C. 484, 483,) and its inhabitants were removed to Syracuse, and Epicharmus among them. The prime of his life, and the most flourishing period of his art, are included in the reign of Hiero, (Ol. 75, 3. to Ol. 78, 2. B.C.

---

* The grammarian Aristophanes of Byzantium, quoted by Athenæus, XIV., p. 659, and Festus, s. v. *Mæson.*

† See Müller's *Dorians,* b. iv. ch. 6. § 9.

‡ Among the standing masks of the Atellana was the *Pappus,* whose name is obviously the Greek πάππος, and reminds us of the Παππωσίληνος, the old leader of the satyrs, in the satyric drama ; the *Maccus,* whose name is explained by the Greek μακκοᾶν ; also the *Simus,* (at least in later times: Sueton. *Galba,* 13,) which was a peculiar epithet of the Satyrs from their flat noses.

§ In Hephæstion, *Encheir.* p. 45.

478, 467.) These chronological data are sufficient to show that the
tendency of Epicharmus' comedy could not be political. The safety
and dignity of a ruler like Hiero would have been alike incompatible
with such a licence of the stage. It does not, however, follow from this,
that the plays of Epicharmus did not touch upon or perhaps give a complete picture of the great events of the time and the circumstances of the
country; and in fact we can clearly point out such references to the
events of the day in several of the fragments: but the comedies of Epicharmus did not, like those of Aristophanes, take a part in the contests
of political factions and tendencies, nor did they select some particular
political circumstance of Syracuse to be praised as fortunate, while they
represented what was opposed to it as miserable and ruinous. The
comedy of Epicharmus has a general relation to the affairs of mankind:
it ridicules the follies and perversities which certain forms of education had introduced into the social life of man; and a considerable element in it was a vivid representation of particular classes and persons
from common life; a large number of Epicharmus' plays seem to have
been comedies of character, such as his "Peasant," ('Αγρωστῖνος,) and
"the Ambassadors to the Festival," (Θεᾶροι;) we are positively informed
that Epicharmus was the first to bring on the stage the Parasite and the
Drunkard,—characters which Crates worked up for Athenian comedy.
Epicharmus was also the first to use the name of the Parasite,* which
afterwards became so common in Greek and Roman plays, and it is
likely that the rude, merry features with which Plautus has drawn this
class of persons may, in their first outlines, be traceable to Epicharmus.†
The Syracusan poet no doubt showed in the invention of such characters
much of that shrewdness for which the Dorians were distinguished more
than the other Greek tribes; careful and acute observations of mankind
are compressed into a few striking traits and nervous expressions, so that
we seem to see through the whole man though he has spoken only a few
words. But in Epicharmus this quality was combined in a very peculiar
manner with a striving after philosophy. Epicharmus was a man of a
serious cast of mind, variously and profoundly educated. He belonged
originally to the school of physicians at Cos, who derived their art from
Æsculapius. He had been initiated by Arcesas, a scholar of Pythagoras,
into the peculiar system of the Pythagorean philosophy; and his comedies

---

* In the Attic drama of Eupolis the parasites of the rich Callias appeared as
κόλακις; but the fact that they constituted the chorus rendered it impossible that
they could be made a direct object of comic satire. Alexis, of the middle comedy,
was the first who brought the *parasite* (under this name) on the stage.

    † Gelasime, salve.—Non id est nomen mihi.—
        Certo mecastor id fuit nomen tibi.—
        Fuit disertim; verum id usu perdidi;
        Nunc Miccotrogus nomine ex vero vocor.
                   Plaut. Stich. act 1. sc. 3.
The name *Miccotrogus*, by which the parasite in the preceding passage calls
himself, is not Attic but Doric, and therefore is perhaps derived from Epicharmus.

abounded in philosophical aphorisms,* not merely, as one might at first expect, on notions and principles of morality, but also on metaphysical points—God and the world, body and soul, &c.; where it is certainly difficult to conceive how Epicharmus interwove these speculative discourses into the texture of his comedies. Suffice it to say, we see that Epicharmus found means to connect a representation of the follies and absurdities of the world in which he lived, with profound speculations on the nature of things; whence we may infer how entirely different his manner was from that of the · Athenian comedy.

With this general ethical and philosophical tendency we may easily reconcile the *mythical* form, which we find in most of the comedies of Epicharmus.† Mythical personages have general and formal features, free from all accidental peculiarities, and may therefore be made the best possible basis of the principles and results, the symptoms and criteria of good and bad characters. Did we but possess the comedy of the Dorians, and those portions of the old and middle comedy (especially the latter) which are so closely connected with it, we should be able to discern clearly what we can now only guess from titles and short fragments, that mythology thus treated was just as fruitful a source of materials for comedy as for the ideal world of the tragic drama. No doubt, the whole system of gods and heroes must have been reduced to a lower sphere of action in order to suit them to the purposes of comedy: the anthropomorphic treatment of the gods must necessarily have arrived at its last stage; the deities must have been reduced to the level of common life with all its civic and domestic relations, and must have exhibited the lowest and most vulgar inclinations and passions. Thus the insatiable gluttony of Hercules was a subject which Epicharmus painted in vivid colours;‡ in another place,§ a marriage feast among the gods was represented as extravagantly luxurious; a third, " Hephæstus, or the Revellers,"‖ exhibited the quarrel of the fire-god with his mother Hera as a mere family brawl, which is terminated very merrily by Bacchus, who, when the incensed son has left Olympus, invites him to a banquet, makes him sufficiently drunk, and then conducts him back in triumph to Olympus, in the midst of a tumultuous band of revellers. The most lively view which we still have of this mythological comedy is

---

* Epicharmus himself says in some beautiful verses quoted by Diogenes Laertius, III. § 17, that one of his successors would one day surpass all other speculators by adopting his sayings in another form, without metre. It is perhaps not unlikely that the philosophical anthology which was in vogue under the name of Epicharmus, and which Ennius in his *Epicharmus* imitated in trochaic tetrameters, was an excerpt from the comedies of Epicharmus, just as the Gnomology, which we have under the name of Theognis, was a set of extracts from his Elegies.

† Of 35 titles of his comedies, which have come down to us, 17 are borrowed from mythological personages. Grysar, *de Doriensium Comœdia*, p. 274.

‡ In his *Busiris*.   § In the *Marriage of Hebe*.

‖ Ἥφαιστος ἢ Κωμασταί.

furnished by the scenes in Aristophanes which seem to have the same
tone and feeling: such as that in which Prometheus appears as the mal-
content and intriguer in Olympus, and points out the proper method of
depriving the gods of their sovereignty; and then the embassy of the
three gods, when Hercules, on smelling the roasted birds, forgets the
interests of his own party, and the voice of the worst of the three ambassadors constitutes the majority; this shows us what striking pictures for
situations of common life and common relations might be borrowed from
the supposed condition of the gods. At any rate, we may also see from
this how the comic treatment of mythology differed from that in the
satyric drama. In the latter, the gods and heroes were introduced
among a class of beings in whom a rude, uncultivated mode of life predominated: in the former they descended to social life, and were
subject to all the deficiencies and infirmities of human society.

§ 6. The Sicilian comedy in its artistic developement preceded the
Attic by about a generation; yet the transition to the *middle Attic
comedy*, as it is called, is easier from Epicharmus than from Aristophanes,
who appears very unlike himself in the play which tends towards the
form of the middle comedy. This branch of comedy belongs to a time when
the democracy was still moving in unrestrained freedom, though the
people had no longer such pride and confidence in themselves as to ridicule from the stage their rulers and the recognized principles of state
policy, and at the same time to prevent themselves from being led astray
by such ridicule. The unfortunate termination of the Peloponnesian war
had damped the first fresh vigour of the Athenian state; freedom and
democracy had been restored to the Athenians, and even a sort of maritime supremacy; but their former energy of public life had not been
restored along with these things; there were too many weaknesses and
defects in all parts of their political condition,—in their finances, in the
war-department, in the law-courts. The Athenians, perhaps, were well
aware of this, but they were too indolent and fond of pleasure to set
about in earnest to free themselves from these inconveniences. Under such
circumstances, satire and ridicule, such as Aristophanes indulged in,
would have been quite intolerable, for it would no longer have pointed
out certain shadows in a bright and glorious picture, but would have
exhibited one dark picture without a single redeeming ray of light, and
so would have lacked all the cheerfulness of comedy. Accordingly, the
comedians of this time took that general moral tendency which we have
pointed out in the Megarian comedy and in all that is connected with it;
they represented the ludicrous absurdities of certain classes and conditions in society,* and in their diction kept close to the language of common

* A bragging cook, a leading personage in middle comedy, was the chief character
in the *Æolosicon* of Aristophanes. We may infer what influence the Megarian
and Sicilian comedy had in the formation of regular standing characters, from the

life, which prevails much more uniformly in their plays than in those of Aristophanes, with the exception of some few passages, where it is interrupted by parodies of epic and tragic poetry.* These comedians were not altogether without a basis of personal satire; but this was no longer directed against influential men, the rulers of the people; † or, if it touched them at all, it was not on account of their political character, or of any principles approved by the bulk of the people. On the contrary, the middle comedy cultivated a narrower field of its own,—the department of literary rivalship. The poems of the middle comedy were rich in ridicule of the Platonic Academy, of the newly revived sect of the Pythagoreans, of the orators and rhetoricians of the day, and of the tragic and epic poets: they sometimes even took a retrospective view, and subjected to their criticism anything which they thought weak or imperfect in the poems of Homer. This criticism was totally different from that directed by Aristophanes against Socrates, which was founded exclusively upon moral and practical views; the judgments of the middle comedy considered everything in a literary point of view, and, if we may reason from individual instances, were directed solely against the character of the writings of the persons criticized. In the transition from the old to the middle comedy we may discern at once the great revolution which had taken place in the domestic history of Athens, when the Athenians, from a people of politicians, became a nation of literary men; when, instead of pronouncing judgment upon the general politics of Greece, and the law-suits of their allies, they judged only of the genuineness of the Attic style and of good taste in oratory; when it was no longer the opposition of the political ideas of Themistocles and Cimon, but the contests of opposing schools of philosophers and rhetoricians, which set all heads in motion. This great change was not fully accomplished till the time of Alexander's successors; but the middle comedy stands as a guide-post, clearly pointing out the way to this consummation. The frequency of mythical subjects in the comedies of this class ‡ has the same grounds as in the Sicilian comedy; for the object in both was to clothe general delineations of character in a mythical form. Further than this, we must admit that our conceptions of the middle comedy are somewhat vacillating and uncertain; this arises from the constitution of the middle comedy itself, which is rather a transition

fact that Pollux (*Onom.* IV., § 146, 148, 150) names the *Sicilian parasite* and the scullion *Mæson* among the masks of the new comedy, (according to the restoration by Meineke, *Hist. Crit. Com. Græc.*, p. 664, comp. above, § 4.)

* Hence we see why the Scholiast, in the *Plutus*, 515, recognizes the character of the middle comedy in the epic tone of the passage.

† On the contrary, these comedians considered ludicrous representations of foreign rulers as quite allowable; thus the *Dionysius* of Eubulus was directed against the Sicilian tyrants, and the *Dionysalexandrus* of the younger Cratinus against Alexander of Pheræ. Similarly, in later times, Menander satirized Dionysius, tyrant of Heraclea, and Philemon king Magas of Cyrene.

‡ Meineke (*Hist. Crit. Com. Græc.*, p. 283, foll.) gives a long list of such mythical comedies.

state than a distinct species. Consequently, we find, along with many
features resembling the old comedy, also some peculiarities of the new.
Aristotle indeed speaks only of an old and a new comedy, and does not
mention the middle comedy as distinct from the new.

The poets of the middle comedy are also very numerous; they occupy
the interval between Ol. 100. b.c. 380, and the reign of Alexander.
Among the earliest of them we find the sons of Aristophanes, *Araros* and
Philippus, and the prolific *Eubulus*, who flourished about Ol. 101. b.c.
376: then follows *Anaxandrides*, who is said to have been the first to
introduce into comedy the stories of love and seduction, which afterwards
formed so large an ingredient in it *—so that we have here another
reference to the new comedy, and the first step in its subsequent developement. Then we have *Amphis* and *Anaxilaus*, both of whom made
Plato the butt of their wit; the younger *Cratinus; Timocles*, who ridiculed the orators Demosthenes and Hyperides; still later, *Alexis*, one of
the most productive, and at the same time one of the most eminent of
these poets : his fragments, however, show a decided affinity to the new
comedy, and he was a contemporary of Menander and Philemon.†
Antiphanes began to exhibit as early as 383 b.c.; his comedies, however,
were of much the same kind with those of Alexis: he was by far the
most prolific of the poets of the middle comedy, and was distinguished
by his redundant wit and inexhaustible invention. The number of his
pieces, which amounted to 300, and according to some authorities ex-
ceeded that number, proves that the comedians of this time no longer
contended, like Aristophanes, with single pieces, and only at the Lenæa
and great Dionysia, but either composed for the other festivals, or, what
seems to us the preferable opinion, produced several pieces at the same
festival. ‡

§ 7. These last poets of the *middle comedy* were contemporaries of the
writers of the *new comedy*, who rose up as their rivals, and were only
distinguished from them by following their new tendency more decidedly
and more exclusively. *Menander* was one of the first of these poets, (he
flourished at the time immediately succeeding the death of Alexander,§)
and he was also the most perfect of them, which will not surprise us if
we consider the middle comedy as a sort of preparation for the new.||

* The *Cocalus* of Aristophanes (Araros) contains, according to Platonius, a
scene of seduction and recognition of the same kind with those in the comedies of
Menander.

† It appears by the fragment of the *Hypobolimæus*, (Athen. XI. p. 502. b.
Meineke *Hist. Crit. Com. Græc.* p. 315.)

‡ Concerning Antiphanes, see Clinton, *Philol. Mus.* I. p. 558 foll., and Meineke,
Hist. Crit. Com. Gr. p. 304—40. It appears from the remarks of Clinton, p. 607,
and Meineke, p. 305, that the passage attributed by Athenæus IV. p. 156. c., to
Antiphanes, in which king Seleucus is mentioned, is probably by another comic poet.

§ Menander brought out his first piece when he was still a young man (Ἰφηβος),
in Ol. 114, 3. b.c. 322, and died as early as Ol. 122, 1. b.c. 291.

|| According to *Anon. de comœdia*, Menander was specially instructed in his act
by Alexis.

Philemon came forward rather earlier than Menander, and survived him many years; he was a great favourite with the Athenians, but was always placed after Menander by those who knew them both.* These are followed by *Philippides*, a contemporary of Philemon;† by *Diphilus* of Sinope,‡ who was somewhat later; by *Apollodorus* of Gela, a contemporary of Menander, *Apollodorus* of Carystus, who was in the following generation,§ and by a considerable number of poets, more or less worthy to be classed with these.

Passing here from the middle comedy to the new, we come at once to a clearer region; here the Roman imitations, combined with the numerous and sometimes considerable fragments, are sufficient to give us a clear conception of a comedy of Menander in its general plan and in its details: a person who possessed the peculiar talents requisite for such a task, and had acquired by study the acquaintance with the Greek language and the Attic subtlety of expression necessary for the execution of it, might without much difficulty restore a piece of Menander's, so as to replace the lost original. The comedy of the Romans must not be conceived as merely a learned and literary imitation of the Greek: it formed a living union with the Greek comedy, by a transfer to Rome of the whole Greek stage, not by a mere transmission through books; and in point of time too there is an immediate and unbroken connexion between them. For although the period at which the Greek new comedy flourished followed immediately upon the death of Alexander, yet the first generation was followed by a second, as Philemon the son followed Philemon the father, and comic writing of less merit and reputation most probably continued till a late period to provide by new productions for the amusement of the people; so that when Livius Andronicus first appeared before the Roman public with plays in imitation of the Greek (A.U.C. 514. B.C. 240), the only feat which he performed was, to attempt in the language of Rome what many of his contemporaries were in the habit of dong in the Greek language; at any rate, the plays of Menander and Philemon were the most usual gratification which an educated audience sought for in the theatres of Greek states, as well in Asia as in Italy. By viewing the case in this way, we assume at once the proper position for surveying the Latin comedians in all their relations to the Greek, which are so peculiar that they can only be developed under these limited historical conditions. For to take the two cases, which seem at first sight the most obvious and natural; namely, first, that *translations* of the plays of Menander,

---

* Menander said to him, when he had won the prize from him in a dramatic contest, " Philemon, do you not blush to conquer me?" Aul. Gell. *N.A.*, XVII. 4.

† According to Suidas he came forward Ol. 111., still earlier than Philemon.

‡ Sinope was at that time the native city of three comedians, Diphilus, Dionysius, and Diodorus, and also of the cynic philosopher Diogenes. It must have been the fashion at Sinope to derive proper names from Zeus, the Zeus Chthonius or Serapis of Sinope.

§ According to the inferences in Meineke's *Hist. Crit. Com. Græc.*, p. 459, 462.

Philemon, &c., were submitted to the educated classes at Rome ; or
secondly, that people attempted by *free imitations* to transplant these
pieces into a Roman soil, and then to suit them to the tastes and under-
standings of the Roman people by romanizing them, not merely in all
the allusions to national customs and regulations, but also in their spirit
and character : neither of these two alternatives was adopted, but
the Roman comedians took a middle course, in consequence of which
these plays *became Roman* and yet *remained perfectly Greek*.   In
other words : in the Greek comedy (or *comœdia palliata*, as it was called)
of the Romans, the training of Greece in general, and of Athens in particular, has extended itself to Rome, and has compelled the Romans, so
far as they wished to participate in that, in which all the educated world
at that time participated, to acquiesce in the outward forms and conditions
of this drama ;—in its Greek costume and Athenian locality ; to adopt
Attic life as a model of social ease and familiarity ; and (to speak plainly)
to consider themselves for an hour or two as mere barbarians,—and,
in fact, the Roman comedians occasionally speak of themselves and their
countrymen as *barbari*.[*]

It is necessary that we should premise these observations, (however
much they may seem chronologically misplaced,) in order to justify the
use which we purpose to make of Plautus and Terence.   The Roman
comedians prepared the Greek dish for the Roman palate in a different
manner according to their own peculiar tastes ; for example, Plautus
seasoned it with coarse and powerful condiments, Terence on the other
hand with moderate and delicate seasoning ;[†] but it still remained the
Attic dish : the scene brought before the Roman public was Athens in
the time of those Macedonian rulers who are called the *Diadochi* and
Epigoni.[‡]

§ 8. Consequently, the scene was Athens after the downfall of its
political freedom and power, effected by the battle of Chæronea, and still
more by the Lamian war : but it was Athens, still the city of cities, overflowing with population, flourishing with commerce, and strong in its
navy, prosperous both as a state and in the wealth of many of its individual citizens.[§]   This Athens, however, differed from that of Cimon

---

[*] See Plautus, *Bacchid.* I. 2. 15. *Captivi*. III. 1. 32. IV. 1. 104.   *Trinumm. Prol.*
19.   Festus v. *barbari* and *vapula*.

[†] Yet Plautus is more an imitator and frequently a translator of the Attic comedians than many persons have supposed.   Not to speak of Terence, Cæcilius Statius
has also followed very closely in the steps of Menander.

[‡] So much so, that the most peculiar features of Attic law (as in all that related
to ἐπίκληροι, or heiresses) and of the political relations of Athens (as the κληρουχία
in Lemnos) play an important part in the Roman comedies.

[§] The finances of Athens were to all appearance as flourishing under Lycurgus
(i. e. B.C. 338—326) as under Pericles.   The well-known census under Demetrius
the Phalerian (B.C. 317) gives a proof of the number of citizens and slaves at
Athens.   Even in the days of Demetrius Poliorcetes, Athens had still a great fleet.
In a word, Athens did not want *means* at this time to enable her to command the
respect even of kings ; she only lacked the necessary spirit.

and Pericles much in the same way as an old man weak in body, but full of a love of life, good humoured and self-indulgent, differs from the vigorous middle-aged man at the summit of his bodily strength and mental energy. The qualities which were before singularly united in the Athenian character, namely, resolute bravery and subtlety of intellect, were now entirely disjoined and separated. The former had taken up its abode with the homeless bands of mercenaries who practised war as a handicraft, and it was only on impulses of rare occurrence that the people of Athens gave way to a warlike enthusiasm which was speedily kindled and as speedily quenched. But the excellent understanding and mother-wit of the Athenians, so far as they did not ramble in the schools of the philosophers and rhetoricians, found an object (now that there was so little in politics which could interest or employ the mind) in the occurrences of social life, and in the charm of dissolute enjoyments.

Dramatic poetry now for the first time centered in *love*,* as it has since done among all nations to whom Greek cultivation has descended; but certainly it was not love in those nobler forms to which it has since elevated itself. The seclusion and want of all society in which un-married women lived at Athens (such as we have before described it, in speaking of the poetry of Sappho)† continued to prevail unaltered in the families of the citizens of Athens; according to these customs then, an amour of any continuance with the daughter of a citizen of Athens was out of the question, and never occurs in the fragments and imitations of the comedy of Menander; if the plot of the piece depends on the seduction of an Athenian damsel, this has taken place suddenly and without premeditation, in a fit of drunkenness and youthful lust, generally at one of the *pervigilia*, which the religion of Athens had sanctioned from the earliest times: or some supposed slave or *hetæra*, with whom the hero is desperately in love, turns out to be a well-born Athenian maiden, and marriage at last crowns a connexion entered upon with very different intentions.‡

The intercourse of the young men with the *hetæræ* or courtesans, an intercourse which had always been a reproach to them since the days of Aristophanes,§ had at length become a regular custom with the young people of the better class, whose fathers did not treat them too parsi-moniously. These courtesans, who were generally foreigners or freed-women,‖ possessed more or less education and charms of manner, and in

* Fabula jucundi nulla est sine amore Menandri. Ovid. *Trist.*, II. 370.
† Chap. XIII. § 6.
‡ This is the φθορὰ and the ἀναγνώρισις, which formed the basis of so many of Menander's comedies.
§ See *e. g. Clouds*, 996.
‖ This constitutes the essential distinction between the ἑταίρα and the πόρνη, the latter being a slave of the πορνοβοσκός (ὁ, ἡ, the *leno* or *lena*), although the πόρναι are often ransomed (λύονται) by their lovers, and so rise into the other more honour-able condition.

proportion to these attractions, bound the young people to them with more
or less of constancy and exclusiveness; their lovers found an entertainment in their society which naturally rendered them little anxious to
form a regular matrimonial alliance, especially as the legitimate daughters
of Athenian citizens were still brought up in a narrow and limited
manner, and with few accomplishments. The fathers either allowed
their sons a reasonable degree of liberty to follow their own inclinations
and sow their wild oats, or through parsimony or morose strictness endeavoured 'to withhold from them these indulgencies, in the midst of all
which it often happened that the old man fell into the very same follies
which he so harshly reproved in his son. In these domestic intrigues
the slaves exercised an extraordinary influence: even in Xenophon's
time, favoured by the spirit of democracy, and as it seems almost standing on the same footing with the meaner citizens, they were still more
raised up by the growing degeneracy of manners, and the licence which
universally prevailed. In these comedies, therefore, it often happens
that a slave forms the whole plan of operations in an intrigue; it is his
sagacity alone which relieves his young master from some disagreeable
embarrassment, and helps to put him in possession of the object of his
love: at the same time we are often introduced to rational slaves, who
try to induce their young masters to follow the suggestions of some
sudden better resolution, and free themselves at once from the exactions
of an unreasonable *hetæra*.* No less important are the *parasites*, who,
not to speak of the comic situations in which they are placed by their
resolution to eat without labouring for it, are of great use to the comedian
in their capacity of a sort of dependents on the family: they are brought
into social relations of every kind, and are ready to perform any service
for the sake of a feast. Of the characters who make their appearance
less frequently, we will only speak here of 'the *Bramarbas* or *miles glo-
riosus*. He is no Athenian warrior, no citizen-soldier, like the heroes
of the olden time, but a homeless leader of mercenaries, who enlists men-
at-arms, now for king Seleucus, now for some other crowned general;
who makes much booty with little trouble in the rich provinces of Asia,

---

* As in Menander's *Eunuch*, in the scene of which Persius gives a miniature
copy (*Sat.* V. 161). In this passage Persius has Menander immediately in his
eye, and not the imitation in Terence's *Eunuch*, act i. sc. 1, although Terence's
Phædria, Parmeno, and Thais, correspond to the Chærestratus, Daos, and Chrysis
of Menander. In Menander, however, the young man takes counsel with his
slave at a time when the *hetæra* had shut him out, and on the supposition that she
would invite him to come to her again: in Terence the lover is already invited to
a reconciliation after a quarrel. This results from the adoption by Terence of a
practice common with the Latin comedians, and called *contaminatio;* he has here
combined in one piece two of Menander's comedies, the *Eunuch* and the *Kolax*.
Accordingly he is obliged to take up the thread of the Eunuch somewhat later, in
order to gain more room for the developement of his double plot. In the same
manner the *Adelphi* of Terence is made up from the Γεωργός of Menander and the
Συναποθνήσκοντες of Diphilus.

and is willing to squander it away in lavish extravagance on the amiable
courtesans of Athens; who is always talking of his services, and has
thereby habituated himself to continual boasting and bragging : consequently he is a demi-barbarian, overreached by his parasite and cheated
at pleasure by some clever slave, and with many other traits of this kind
which may easily be derived from the Roman comedies, but can only be
viewed in their right light by placing the character about 100 years
earlier.*

§ 9. This was the world in which Menander lived, and which, according to universal testimony, he painted so truly.   Manifestly, the motives
here rested upon no mighty impulses, no grand ideas.   The strength of
the old Athenian principles and the warmth of national feelings had
gradually grown fainter and weaker till they had melted down into a
sort of philosophy of life, the main ingredients of which were a
natural good temper and forbearance, and a sound mother-wit nurtured
by acute observation ; and its highest principle was that rule of " live
and let live," which had its root in the old spirit of Attic democracy,
and had been developed to the uttermost by the lax morality of subsequent times.†

It is highly worthy of observation, as a hint towards appreciating the
private life of this period, that *Menander* and *Epicurus* were born in
the same year at Athens, and spent their youth together as sharers in the
same exercises (συνέφηβοι) :‡ and an intimate friendship united these
two men, whose characters had much in common.   Though we should
wrong them both if we considered them as slaves to any vulgar sensu-
ality, yet it cannot be doubted that they were both of them deficient in
the inspiration of high moral ideas.   The intention with which each
of them acted was the same : 'to make the most of life as it is, and to
make themselves as agreeable as they could.   They were both too
refined and sensible to take any pleasure in vulgar enjoyments ; Menander knew so well by experience the deceitfulness of these gratifications,
and felt so great a weariness and disgust of their charms, that he had

---

* The ἀλάζων of Theophrastus (*Charact.* 23) has some affinity with the Thraso
of comedy (as Theophrastus's characters in general are related to those of Menander), but he is an Athenian citizen who is proud of his connexion with Macedon,
and not a mercenary soldier.

† The aristocratic constitutions at that time in Greece were connected with a
stricter superintendence of morals (*censura morum*) ; the leading principle of the
Athenian democracy, on the other hand, was to impose no further restraint on the
private life of the citizen than the immediate interests of the state required.   However, the writings of the new comedy were not altogether without personal invectives, and there were still questions with regard to the freedom of the comic stage
(Plutarch *Demetr.* 12. Meineke *Hist. Crit. Com. Græc.* p. 436.)   The Latin comedians also occasionally introduced personal attacks, which were most bitter in the
comedies of Nævius.

‡ Strabo XIV. p. 526.   Meineke, *Menandri et Philemonis fragm.*, p. xxv.

arrived at a sort of passionless rest and moderation;* though it is
possible that in actual life Menander placed his happiness less in the
painless tranquillity which Epicurus sought, than in various kinds of
moderate gratification. It is known how much he gave himself up to
intercourse with the *hetæræ*, not merely with the accomplished Glycera,
but also with the wanton Thais; and his effeminate costume, according
to a well-known story,† offended even Demetrius of Phalerus, the regent
of Athens under Cassander, who however led a sufficiently luxurious
life himself.

Such a philosophy of life as this, which places the *summum bonum*
in a well-based love of self, could very well dispense with the gods,
whom Epicurus transferred to the intermundane regions, because,
according to his natural philosophy, he could not absolutely annihilate
them. Agreeing entirely with his friend on this point, Menander
thought that the gods would have a life of trouble if they had to distribute good and evil for every day.‡ It was on this account that the
philosopher attributed so much to the influence of *chance* in the creation
of the world and the destinies of mankind. Menander also exalts Τύχη
(Fortune) as the sovereign of the world; § but this no longer implies the
saviour daughter of almighty Zeus, but merely the causeless, incalcu-
lable, accidental combinations of things in nature and in the life of man.

It was, however, precisely at such a time as this, when all relations
were dislocated or merged in licentiousness, that comedy possessed a
power, which, though widely different from the angry flashes of the
genius of Aristophanes, perhaps produced in its way more durable
effects: this power was the power of ridicule, which taught people to
dread as folly that which they no longer avoided as vice. This power
was the more effective as it confined its operations to the sphere of
the actual, and did not exhibit the follies which it represented under the
same gigantic and superhuman forms as the old comedy. The old
comedy, in its necessity for invention, *created* forms in which it could
pourtray with most prominent features the characteristics of whole
classes and species of men; the new comedy *took* its forms, in all their
individual peculiarities, from real life, and did not attempt to signify by
them more than individuals of the particular class. || On this account
more importance was attached by the writers of the new comedy to the
invention of plots, and to their dramatic complication and solution,

* The reader will find characteristic expressions of this luxurious philosophy in
Meineke, *Menandri fragm.*, p. 166.
† Phædrus, fab., v. 1.
‡ In a fragment which has recently come to light from the commentary of David
on Aristotle's *Categories*. See Meineke, *Hist. Crit. Com. Græc.*, p. 454.
§ Meineke, *Menandri fragm.*, p. 168.
|| Hence the exclamation : ὦ Μίνανδρι καὶ βίι.

which Menander made the leading object in his compositions: for, while the old comedy set its forms in motion in a very free and unconstrained manner, according as the developement of the fundamental thought required, the new comedy was subject to the laws of probability as established by the progress of ordinary life, and had to invent a story in which all the views of the persons and all the circumstances of their actions resulted from the characters, manners, and relations of the age. The stretch of attention on the part of the spectator which Aristophanes produced by the continued progression in the developement of the comic ideas of his play was effected in the new comedy by the confusion and solution of outward difficulties in the circumstances represented, and by the personal interest felt for the particular characters by the spectators,—an interest closely connected with the illusion of reality.

In this the attentive reader of these observations will readily have perceived how comedy, thus conducted by Menander and Philemon, only completed what Euripides had begun on the tragic stage a hundred years before their time. Euripides, too, deprived his characters of that ideal grandeur which had been most conspicuous in the creations of Æschylus, and gave them more of human weakness, and therefore of apparent individuality. Euripides, too, abandoned the foundation of national principles in ethics and religion on which the old popular morality of the Greeks had been built up, and subjected all relations to a dialectical, and sometimes sophistical mode of reasoning, which very soon led to the lax morality and common sense doctrines which prevailed in the new comedy. Euripides and Menander consequently agree so well in their reasonings and sentences, that in their fragments it would be easy to confuse one with the other; and thus tragedy and comedy, these two forms of the drama which started from such different beginnings, here meet as it were in one point.* The form of the diction also contributed a great deal to this: for as Euripides lowered the poetic tone of tragedy to the ordinary language of polished society, in the same way comedy, and indeed even the middle,† but still more the new, relinquished, on the one hand, the high poetic tone which Aristophanes had aimed at, especially in his choral songs, and, on the other hand, the spirit of caricature and burlesque which is essentially connected with the portraiture of his characters: the tone of polished conversation‡ predominates in all the pieces of the new comedy; and in this Menander gave a greater freedom and liveliness to the recitations of his

---

* Philemon was so warm an admirer of Euripides, that he declared he would at once destroy himself, in order to see Euripides in the other world, provided he could convince himself that departed spirits preserved their life and understanding. See Meineke, *Men. et Philem. Rel.*, p. 410.

† According to *Anonymus de Comœdia*, p. xxviii.

‡ This is particularly mentioned by Plutarch (*Aristoph. et Menandri compar.*, c. 2.)

actors by the looser structure of his sentences and the weaker connexion
of his periods; whereas Philemon's pieces, by their more connected and
periodic style, were better suited for the closet than for the stage.* The
Latin comedians, Plautus, for instance, gave a great deal more of burlesque than they found in their models, availing themselves perhaps of
the Sicilian comedy of Epicharmus, as well as of the comedy of their
own country. The elevated poetic tone must have been lost with the
choruses, of which we have no sure traces even in the middle comedy;†
the connexion of lyric and dramatic poetry was limited to the employment by the actors of lyric measures of different kinds, and they expressed their feelings at the moment by singing these lyrical pieces, and
accompanying them with lively gesticulations: in this the model was
rather the monodies of Euripides than the lyrical passages in Aristophanes.

We have now brought down the history of the Attic drama from
Æschylus to *Menander*, and in naming these two extreme points of
the series through which dramatic poetry developed itself, we cannot
refrain from reminding our readers what a treasure of thought and life
is here unfolded to us; what remarkable changes were here effected,
not only in the forms of poetry, but in the inmost recesses of the constitution of the Greek mind; and what a great and significant portion
of the history of our race is here laid before us in the most vivid
delineations.

CHAPTER XXX.

§ 1. The Dithyramb becomes the chief form of Athenian lyric poetry. Lasus of
　　Hermione. § 2. New style of the dithyramb introduced by Melanippides. Phi-
　　loxenus. Cinesias. Phrynis. Timotheus. Polyeidus. § 3. Mode of producing
　　the new dithyramb: its contents and character. § 4. Reflective lyric poetry.
　　§ 5. Social and political elegies. The *Lyde* of Antimachus essentially different
　　from these. § 6. Epic poetry. Panyasis, Chœrilus, Antimachus.

§ 1. THE Drama was so well adapted to reflect the thoughts and
feelings of the people of Attica in the mirror of poetry, that other sorts
of metrical composition fell completely into the back-ground, and for

---

* According to a remark of the so named *Demetrius Phaler. de Elocut.*, § 193.
† According to Platonius, the middle comedy had no parabases, because there
was no chorus. The *Æolosicon* was quite without choral songs. The new comedians, in imitation of the older writers, wrote ΧΟΡΟΣ at the end of the acts; probably the pause was filled up by the performance of a flute-player. At any rate,
such was the custom at Rome. Evanthius (*de Comœd.*, p. lv. in Westerton's
Terence) seems to mean the same.

the public in general assumed the character rather of isolated and momentary gratifications than that of a poetic expression of prevailing sentiments and principles.

However, *Lyric poetry* was improved in a very remarkable manner, and struck out tones which seized with new power upon the spirit of the age. This was principally effected by the *new Dithyramb*, the cradle and home of which was Athens, before all the cities of Greece, even though some of the poets who adopted this form were not born there.

As we have remarked above,* LASUS of Hermione, the rival of Simonides, and the teacher of Pindar, in those early days exhibited his dithyrambs chiefly at Athens, and even in his poems the dithyrambic rhythm had gained the greater freedom by which it was from thenceforth characterized. Still the dithyrambs of Lasus were not generically different from those of Pindar, of which we still possess a beautiful fragment. This dithyramb was designed for the vernal Dionysia at Athens, and it really seems to breathe the perfumes and smile with the brightness of spring.† The rhythmical structure of the fragment is bold and rich, and a lively and almost violent motion prevails in it; ‡ but this motion is subjected to the constraint of fixed laws, and all the separate parts are carefully incorporated in the artfully constructed whole. We also see from this fragment that the strophes of the dithyrambic ode were already made very long; from principles, however, which will be stated in the sequel, we must conclude that there were antistrophes corresponding to these strophes.

§ 2. The dithyramb assumed a new character in the hands of MELANIPPIDES of Melos. He was maternal grandson of the older Melanippides, who was born about Ol. 65. B.C. 520, and was contemporary with Pindar; § the younger and more celebrated Melanippides lived for a long period with Perdiccas, king of Macedon, who reigned from about Ol. 81, 2. B.C. 454, to Ol. 91, 2. B.C. 414; consequently, before and during the greater part of the Peloponnesian war. The comic poet Pherecrates (who, like Aristophanes, was in favour of maintaining the old simple music as an essential part of the old-fashioned morality) considers the corruption of the ancient musical modes as having commenced with him. Closely connected with this change is the increasing importance of instrumental music; in consequence of which the flute-players, after the time of Melanippides, no longer received their hire

---

* Chap. XIV. § 14.   † See above, Chap. XIV. § 7.

‡ The pæonic species of rhythms, to which the ancients especially assign " the splendid," (τὸ μεγαλοπρεπὲς,) is the prevailing one in this fragment.

§ That the younger Melanippides is the person with whom, according to the celebrated verses of Pherecrates, (Plutarch *de Musica*, 30. Meineke *Fr. Com. Gr.*, vol. II. p. 326,) the corruption of music begins, is clear, partly from the direct statement of Suidas, partly from his chronological relation to Cinesias and Philoxenus. The celebrated Melanippides was also the contemporary of Thucydides, (Marcellin. *V. Thucyd.* § 29,) and of Socrates, (Xenoph. *Mem.*, I, 4, § 3.)

as mere secondary persons and assistants, from the poets themselves, but were paid immediately by the managers of the festival.*

Melanippides was followed by PHILOXENUS of Cythera, first his slave and afterwards his pupil, who is ridiculed by Aristophanes in his later plays, and especially in the *Plutus*.† He lived, at a later period, at the court of Dionysius the elder, and is said to have taken all sorts of liberties with the tyrant, who sometimes indulged in poetry as an amateur; but he had to pay for this distinction by confinement to the stone-quarries at Syracuse, when the tyrant was in a bad humour. He died Ol. 100, 1. B.C. 380.‡ His Dithyrambs enjoyed the greatest reputation all over Greece, and it is remarkable that while Aristophanes speaks of him as a bold innovator, Antiphanes, the poet of the middle comedy, praises his music as already the genuine style of music, and calls Philoxenus himself, " a god among men;" whereas he calls the music and lyric poetry *of his own time* a flowery style of composition, which adorns itself with foreign melodies. §

In the series of the corrupters of music, Pherecrates, in the passage already quoted, mentions, next to Melanippides, CINESIAS, whom Aristophanes also ridicules about the middle of the Peloponnesian war,‖ on account of his pompous, and at the same time empty diction, and also for his rhythmical innovations. " Our art," he there says, " has its origin in the clouds·: for the splendid passages of the dithyrambs must be aereal, and obscure; azure-radiant, and wing-wafted." Plato¶ designedly brings forward Cinesias as a poet who obviously attached no importance to making his hearers better, but only sought to please the greater number : just as his father *Meles*, who sang to the harp, had wished only to please the common people, but, as Plato sarcastically adds, had done just the reverse, and had only shocked the ears of his audience.

Next to Cinesias, PHRYNIS is arraigned by the personification of Music, who comes forward as the accuser in the lines of Pherecrates, of being one of her worst tormentors, " who had quite annihilated her with his twisting and turnings, since he had twelve modes on five strings." This Phrynis was a later offshoot of the Lesbian school ; he was a singer to the harp, who was born at Mitylene, and won his first victory at the musical contests which Pericles had introduced at the Panathenæa ;** he flourished before and during the Peloponnesian war. The alteration in the old nomes of Terpander, which originally formed the conventional basis of harp-music, is attributed to him. ††

---

* Plutarch, *de Mus.* § 30.   † Aristoph. *Plut.* 290 ; and see *Schol.*
‡ Fifty-five years old. *Marm. Par. ep.* 69.   § Athen. XIV. p. 643, D.
‖ *Birds*, 1372. Comp. *Clouds*, 332. *Peace*, 832.   ¶ *Gorgias*, p. 501, D.
** 'Επὶ Καλλίου ἄρχοντος. *Schol. Clouds*, 976. But no Callias answers to the time when Pericles was agonothetes, and built the Odeium, (about Ol. 84. Plutarch, *Peric!.* 13,) and it is probable that we should substitute the archon Callimachus (Ol. 83, 3.) for Callias.   †† Plutarch, *de Mus.* 6.

TIMOTHEUS of Miletus* formed himself after the model of Phrynis ; at a later period he gained the victory over his master in the musical contests, and raised himself to the highest rank among dithyrambic poets. He is the last of the musical artists censured by Pherecrates, and died in extreme old age in Ol. 105, 4. B.C. 357.† Although the Ephors at Sparta are said to have taken from his harp four of its eleven strings, Greece in general received his innovations in music with the most cordial approbation ; he was one of the most popular musicians of his time. The branches of poetry, which he worked out in the spirit of his own age, were in general the same which Terpander cultivated 400 years before, namely, Nomes, ‡ Proems, and Hymns.   There were still some antique forms which he too was obliged to observe ; for instance, the hexameter verse was not quite given up by Timotheus in his nomes ; but he recited them in the same manner as the Dithyramb, and mixed up this metre with others. §   The branch of poetry which he chiefly cultivated, and which gave its colour to all the others, was undoubtedly the Dithyramb.

Timotheus, too, was worsted, if not before the tribunal of impartial judges, at least in the favour of the public, by POLYEIDUS, whose scholar Philotas also won the prize from Timotheus in a musical contest. ‖ Polyeidus was also regarded as one of those whose artificial innovations were injurious to music, but he also gained a great reputation among the Greeks.   There was nothing which so much delighted the crowded audiences which flocked to the theatres throughout Greece as the Dithyrambs of Timotheus and Polyeidus. ¶

Besides these poets and musicians there was still a long series of others, among whom we may name ION of Chios, who was also a favourite dithyrambic poet ;** DIAGORAS of Melos, the notorious sceptic ;†† the highly-gifted LICYMNIUS of Chios, (whose age is not accurately known ;) CREXUS, also accused of innovations ; and TELESTES of Selinus, a poetic

* See, besides the better known passages, Aristot. *Metaphys.* A. Ἴλαττον, c. 1.

† *Marm. Par.* 76.   Suidas perhaps places his death most correctly at the age of 97.

‡ Steph. Byz. v. Μίλητος, attributes to him 18 books of νόμοι κιθαρῳδικοί, in 8,000 verses ; where the expression ἴση is not to be taken strictly to signify the hexameter, although this metre was mixed up in them.

§ Plut. *de Mus.* 4.   Timotheus's Nome, " the Persians," began ; Κλεινὸν ἐλευθερίας τεύχων μέγαν Ἑλλάδι κόσμον, Pausan. VIII. 50, § 3.

‖ Athenæus, VIII. p. 352, B. Comp. Plutarch, *de Mus.* 21.   It is clear that he is not the same as the tragedian and sophist Polyeidus, mentioned in Aristotle's *Poetic.*   Aristotle would hardly have given the name ὁ σοφιστὴς to a dithyrambic poet whose pursuit was chiefly the study of music.

¶ In a Cretan decree, (*Corp. Inscr. Gr.* N. 305,) one Menecles of Teos is praised for having often played on the harp at Cnossus after the style of Timotheus, Polyeidus, and the old Cretan poets (chap. XII. § 9).

** Comp. Chap. VI. § 2.

†† The most important fragments of his lyric poems are given by the Epicurean, Phædrus, in the papyri brought from Herculaneum (*Herculanensia,* ed. Drummond et Walpole, p. 164).

opponent of Melanippides,* who gained a victory at Athens in Ol. 94, 3.
B.C. 401.

§ 3. It is far more important, however, to obtain a clear conception
of the more recent Dithyramb in all its peculiarities. This we shall be
better able to do by first establishing some of the main points of the
question.

With regard to the *mode of exhibition*, the Dithyrambs at Athens,
during the Peloponnesian war, were still represented by choruses
furnished by the ten tribes for the Dionysian festivals; consequently,
the dithyrambic poets were also called Cyclic chorus-teachers:† but the
more liberty they gave to the metre, the more various their rhythmical
alterations, so much the more difficult was the exhibition by means of a
complete chorus; and so much the more common it became to get the
Dithyramb performed by private amateurs.‡ The Dithyramb also entirely gave up the antistrophic repetition of the same metres, and moved
on in rhythms which depended entirely on the humour and caprice of
the poet;§ it was particularly characterized by certain runs by way of
prelude, which were called ἀναβολαί, and which are much censured by
strict judges, || but doubtless were listened to with avidity by the public
in general. In this the poet had nothing to hinder him from passing
from one musical note to another, or from combining various rhythms in the
same poem ; so that at last all the constraints of metre seemed to vanish,
and poetry in its very highest flight seemed to meet the opposite extreme
of prose, as the old critics remark.

At the same time the Dithyramb assumed a descriptive, or, as Aristotle
says, a *mimetic* character.¶ The natural phenomena which it described
were imitated by means of tunes and rhythms, and the pantomimic gesticulations of the actors, (as in the antiquated Hyporcheme) ; and this was
very much aided by a powerful instrumental accompaniment, which
sought to represent with its loud full tones the raging elements, the voices
of wild beasts, and other sounds.**

With regard to the *contents* or subject of this dithyrambic poetry, in
this it was based upon the compositions of Xenocritus, Simonides, and
other old poets, who had taken subjects for the Dithyramb from the

---

* Athen. XIV. p. 616, E, relates, in very pretty verses, a contest between the
two poets, on the question whether Minerva had rejected the flute-accompaniment.
† Aristoph. *Birds*, 1403.
‡ Aristotle speaks of this alteration, *Problem.* 19, 15. Comp. *Rhetor.* III. 9.
§ ἀπολελυμένα.
|| ἡ μακρὰ ἀναβολὴ τῷ ποιήσαντι κακίστη: an hexameter with a peculiar synizesis.
¶ This is called μεταβολή. The fragments of the dithyrambic poets consequently
contain also many pieces in simple Doric rhythms.
** Plato (*Resp.* p. 396) alludes to this imitation of storms, roaring torrents, lowing
herds, &c., in the Dithyrambs. A parasite wittily observed of one of these storm-
dithyrambs of Timotheus, that " he had seen greater storms, than those which
Timotheus made, in many a kettle of boiling water." Athen. VIII. p. 338, A.

ancient *heroic mythology*.* The Dithyrambs of Melanippides announce
this even by their titles, such as *Marsyas*, (in which, by a modification
of the legend, Athena invents the flute, and on her throwing it away it
is taken up by Marsyas,) *Persephone*, and the *Danaides*. The *Cyclops*
of Philoxenus was in great repute; in this the poet, who was well known
in Sicily, introduced the beautiful Sicilian story of the love of the Cyclops
Polyphemus for the sea-nymph Galatea, who on account of the beautiful
Acis rejects his suit, till at last he takes deadly vengeance on his successful rival. From the verses in Aristophanes in which Philoxenus is parodied,† we may pretty well see in what spirit this subject was treated.
The Cyclops was represented as a harmless monster, a good-natured
Caliban, who roams about the mountains followed by his bleating sheep
and goats as if they were his children, and collects wild herbs in his
wallet, and then half-drunk lays himself down to sleep in the midst of
his flocks. In his love he becomes even poetical, and comforts himself
for his rejection with songs which he thinks quite beautiful: even his
lambs sympathize with his sorrows and bleat longingly for the fair Galatea. ‡ In this whole poem (the subject of which Theocritus took up at
a later period and with better taste formed it into an Idyll §) the ancients
discerned covert allusions to the connexion of the poet with Dionysius,
the poetizing tyrant of Sicily, who is said to have deprived Philoxenus of
the object of his love. If we add to this the statement that Timotheus'
Dithyramb, " the travails of Semele," ‖ passed with the ancients for an
indecent and unimaginative representation of such a scene,¶ we shall have
the means of forming a satisfactory judgment of the general nature of this
new Dithyramb. There was no unity of thought; no one tone pervading
the whole poem, so as to preserve in the minds of the hearers a consistent
train of feelings; no subordination of the story to certain ethical ideas;
no artificially constructed system of verses regulated by fixed laws; but
a loose and wanton play of lyrical sentiments, which were set in motion
by the accidental impulses of some mythical story, and took now one
direction, now another; preferring, however, to seize on such points as
gave room for an immediate imitation in tones, and admitting a mode of
description which luxuriated in sensual charms. Many monodies in the
later tragedies of Euripides, such as Aristophanes ridicules in the " Frogs,"
have this sensual colouring, and in this want of a firm basis to rest upon

* Chap. XIV. § 11. comp. XXI. § 4.
† *Plutus*, 290. The songs of the sheep and goats, which the chorus was there to
bleat forth to please Carion, refer to the imitations of these animals in the Dithyramb.
‡ Hermesianax *Fragm.* v. 74.
§ Theocrit. *Id.* xi., where the reader should consult the scholia.
‖ Σεμέλης ὠδίν.
¶ Of this the witty Stratonicus said, " could she have cried out more piteously,
if she had been bringing forth not a God, but a common mechanic?" Athen. VIII.
p. 352. A. In a similar spirit Polyeidus made Atlas a shepherd in Libya. Tzetz.
on Lycophr. 879.

others, his poem could not possibly have gained the reputation which it enjoyed in ancient times.

§ 6. Here we must resume the thread of our history of *Epic poetry*, which we dropped with Pisander, (chapter IX.) Epic poetry, however, did not slumber in the mean time, but found an utterance in PANYASIS of Halicarnassus, the uncle of Herodotus, (fl. Ol. 78, B.C. 468,[*]) in CHŒRILUS of Samos, a contemporary of Lysander, (about Ol..94, B.C. 404,) and in ANTIMACHUS of Colophon, just mentioned, whose younger days coincide with the old age of Chœrilus :[†] these poets, however, were received by the public with an indifference fully equal to the general attention and admiration which the Homeric poems had excited. The Alexandrian school was the first to bring them into notice, and the critics of this school placed Panyasis and Antimachus, together with Pisander, in the first rank of epic poets. On this account also we have proportionally few fragments of these poets; most of the citations from them are made only for the sake of learned illustrations; but little has come down to us, which could give us a conception of their general style and art.

PANYASIS comprised in his " Hercules " 'a great mass of mythical legends, and was chiefly occupied with painting in romantic colours the adventures of this hero in the most distant regions of the world. The description of the mighty feats of this hero, of his athletic strength˙ and invincible courage, were no doubt relieved or softened down by pictures of a very different kind; such as those, in which Panyasis gave life to a feast where Hercules was present by recounting the pleasant speeches of the valiant banqueters, or painted in warm colours the thraldom of Hercules to Omphale which brought him to Lydia.

In a great epic poem called *Ionica*, Panyasis took for his subject the early history of the Ionians in Asia Minor, and their wanderings and settlements under the guidance of Neleus and others of the descendants of Codrus.

CHŒRILUS of Samos formed the grand plan of exalting in epic poetry the greatest or at least the most joyful event of Greek history, *the expedition of Xerxes, king of Persia, against Greece.* We could not blame this choice, even though we considered the historical epos, properly so called, an unnatural production. But the Persian war was in its leading features an event of such simplicity and grandeur,—the despot of the East leading against the free republics of Greece, countless hosts of people who had no will of their own,—and besides this, the sub-

---

[*] This date is given by Suidas; somewhat later, (about Ol. 82,) Panyasis was put to death by Lygdamis, the tyrant of Halicarnassus, whom Herodotus afterwards expelled.

[†] When Lysander was in Samos as the conqueror of Athens, Chœrilus was then with him, and in the musical contests which Lysander established there, Antimachus, son of Niceratus, from Heraclea, then a young man, was one of the defeated poets. Plutarch, *Lysander*, 18.

A

LIST OF THE SOCIETY'S MAPS,

ALREADY PUBLISHED,

Price *Sixpence* Each, or *Ninepence* Coloured.

(Those marked thus * may be obtained at the Society's Office, the others at
Messrs. Baldwin and Cradock's, Paternoster Row.)

*The Stars, in Six Maps.
*The World, in Six Maps.
The Islands in the Atlantic, 1 Part

*The Islands in the Pacific, 2 Maps
Principal Rivers in the World, 1

EUROPE.

	Maps		Maps
Europe, General Map	1	Spain, in	3
England, in	5	Portugal	1
Do. (Canals and Railways)	1	*Spain and Portugal, Ancient	1
Ancient Britain, in	2	*Do. do., Modern	1
Scotland, in	3	Germany, in	4
*Ireland, in	2	*Do. General Map	1
France in Departments	3	Austrian Dominions, in	3
Do. Provinces	1	Poland	1
Do. Ancient	1	Denmark, Sweden, Norway	
*Netherlands	1	and Russia in Europe, in	11
*Switzerland	1	*Russia, General Map	1
Italy, in	3	Turkey and Greece, in	3
Do. Ancient, in	3	Ancient Greece, Macedonia,	
*Italy, General Map	1	and Thrace, in	3
Corsica, Sardinia, Malta, &c.	1		

ASIA.

	Maps		Maps
*Asia, General Map	1	*Bokhara, Cabool, &c.	1
*Siberia and Chinese Tartary	1	*The Panjab, with part of	
*Eastern Siberia	1	Afghanistan, Delhi, &c.	1
*Western Siberia	1	India, in	12
Asia Minor	1	China and the Birman Empire	1
Do. Ancient	1	Eastern Islands, or Malay	
Persia	1	Archipelago	1
Do. Ancient	1	Empire of Japan	1

AFRICA.

	Maps		Maps
*General Map of Africa.	1	*Northern Africa, Ancient.	1
Egypt	1	*Western Africa	2
Do. Ancient.	1	Southern do.	1
Northern Africa.	5		

AMERICA AND WEST INDIES.

	Maps		Maps
British North America and United States, in	16	West India Islands, in	2
		South America	3

	Maps		
*AUSTRALIA, General Map.	1	Western Australia and Van Diemen's Land.	1
New South Wales	1		

*New Zealand . . . . . . 1 Map.

PLANS OF CITIES.

	Maps		Maps
Amsterdam	1	Madrid	1
Antwerp	1	Milan	1
Athens.	1	Moscow	1
Berlin	1	Munich	1
*Birmingham	1	Naples.	1
Bordeaux	1	Oporto.	1
Brussels	1	Paris	2
Copenhagen	1	Environs of Paris	1
Dresden	1	*Parma	1
Dublin.	1	St. Petersburgh	1
Environs of Dublin.	1	Pompeii	1
Edinburgh	1	Ancient Rome.	1
*Environs of Edinburgh.	1	Modern Rome.	1
Frankfort.	1	Stockholm	1
Florence	1	*Syracuse Ancient.	1
Genoa	1	Turin	1
Lisbon	1	*Venice	2
Liverpool.	1	Vienna.	1
London	2	Warsaw	1
Environs of London	1	*New York.	1

59, *Lincoln's Inn Fields.*

London: Printed by WILLIAM CLOWES and Sons, Stamford-street.

LIBRARY OF USEFUL KNOWLEDGE.

HISTORY OF THE
LITERATURE OF GREECE.
VOL. II.—PART III.

COMMITTEE.

Chairman—The Right Hon. LORD BROUGHAM, F.R.S., Member of the
National Institute of France.
Vice Chairman—The Right Hon. EARL SPENCER.
Treasurer—JOHN WOOD, Esq.

WM. ALLEN, Esq., F.R. and R.A.S.
CAPTAIN BEAUFORT, R.N. F.R. and R.A.S.
GEORGE BIRKBECK, M.D.
GEORGE BURROWS, M.D.
PETER STAFFORD CAREY, Esq., A.M.
JOHN CONOLLY, M.D.
WILLIAM COULSON, Esq.
R. DAVIS CRAIG, Esq.
THE RIGHT REV. THE BISHOP OF ST. DAVID'S, D.D.
J. F. DAVIS, Esq., F.R.S.
H. T. DE LA BECHE, Esq., F.R.S.
THE RIGHT HON. LORD DENMAN.
SAMUEL DUCKWORTH, Esq.
THE RIGHT REV. THE BISHOP OF DURHAM, D.D.
SIR HY. ELLIS, Prin. Lib. Brit. Mus.
T. F. ELLIS, Esq., A.M., F.R.A.S.
JOHN ELLIOTSON, M.D., F.R.S.
GEORGE EVANS, Esq., M.P.
THOMAS FALCONER, Esq.
I. L. GOLDSMID, Esq., F.R. and R.A.S.
FRANCIS HENRY GOLDSMID, Esq.
B. GOMPERTZ, Esq., F.R. and R.A.S.
J. T. GRAVES, Esq., A.M., F.R.S.
G. B. GREENOUGH, Esq., F.R. and L.S.
SIR EDMUND HEAD, Bart., A.M.
M. D. HILL, Esq., Q.C.
ROWLAND HILL, Esq., F.R.A.S.
RIGHT HON. SIR J. C. HOBHOUSE, Bart., M.P.
THOMAS HODGKIN, M.D.

DAVID JARDINE, Esq., A.M.
HENRY B. KER, Esq.
THOMAS HEWITT KEY, Esq., A.M.
SIR CHARLES LEMON, Bart.
GEORGE C. LEWIS, Esq., A.M.
THOMAS HENRY LISTER, Esq.
JAMES LOCH, Esq., M.P., F.G.S.
GEORGE LONG, Esq., A.M.
HY. MALDEN, Esq, A.M.
ARTHUR T. MALKIN, Esq., A.M.
MR. SERJEANT MANNING.
R. I. MURCHISON, Esq., F.R.S., F.G.S.
THE RIGHT HON. LORD NUGENT.
W. SMITH O'BRIEN, Esq., M.P.
THE RIGHT HON. SIR HY. PARNELL, Bart.
RICHARD QUAIN, Esq.
P. M. ROGET, M.D., Sec. R.S., F.R.A.S.
R. W. ROTHMAN, Esq., A.M.
SIR MARTIN A. SHEE, P.R.A., F.R.S.
SIR GEO. T. STAUNTON, Bart.
JOHN TAYLOR, Esq., F.R.S.
A. T. THOMSON, M.D.
THOMAS VARDON, Esq.
JAMES WALKER, Esq., F.R.S.
HY. WAYMOUTH, Esq.
THOS. WEBSTER, Esq., A.M.
RIGHT HON. LORD WROTTESLEY, A.M., F.R.A'S.
JOHN ASHTON YATES, Esq.

THOMAS COATES, Esq., *Secretary*, 59, Lincoln's Inn Fields.

LONDON:
PUBLISHED BY THE SOCIETY FOR THE DIFFUSION OF
USEFUL KNOWLEDGE,
59, LINCOLN'S INN FIELDS.

No. 346.] *August 1, 1841.* [*Price Sixpence.*

GEOGRAPHY OF AMERICA.

This Work may be obtained, bound in cloth boards, with three illustrative coloured MAPS, price Twelve Shillings.

The Maps may be had separately, price Eighteenpence.

MAPS.

No. XC., containing SOUTH AMERICA, Part VI., and the ISLANDS in the INDIAN OCEAN has been published.

No. XCI., containing Plans of HAMBURGH and GENEVA, will be published in August.

No. XCII. will shortly follow.

POLITICAL PHILOSOPHY.

THE following Numbers of this Series have been already published. The Numbers appear on the 15th of each month, price Sixpence.

No. I.—PRELIMINARY DISCOURSE of the OBJECTS, PLEASURES, and ADVANTAGES of POLITICAL SCIENCE.

Nos. II. and III.—PRINCIPLES OF GOVERNMENT.

No. IV.—ABSOLUTE MONARCHY—EASTERN DESPOTISMS.

No. V.—EASTERN DESPOTISMS (*continued*)—EFFECTS OF ABSOLUTE MONARCHIES.

No. VI.—THE GOVERNMENTS OF CHINA AND JAPAN.

Nos. VII. and VIII.—THE GOVERNMENT OF RUSSIA.

Nos. IX. and X.—THE FEUDAL SYSTEM.

No. XI.—CONSTITUTIONAL MONARCHY.

Nos. XII., XIII., and XIV.—THE FRENCH MONARCHY.

Nos. XV. and XVI.—THE GERMANIC EMPIRE and MONARCHIES.

No. XVII.—THE ITALIAN MONARCHIES, Part I. PAPAL STATES.

No. XIX.—THE ITALIAN MONARCHIES (*continued*) will also be published this month..

59, *Lincoln's Inn Fields.*

ordinate details had been cast into such darkness and obscurity by the infinite multiplication of stories among the Greeks, that it gave room for an absolutely poetic treatment. If Aristotle is right in asserting that poetry is more philosophical than history, because it contains more general truth, it must be admitted that events like the Persian war place themselves on the same footing with poetry, or with a history naturally poetical. Whether Chœrilus, however, conceived this subject in all its grandeur, and considered it with equal liveliness and vigour in its higher and lower relations, cannot now be determined, as the few fragments refer to particulars only, and generally to subordinate details.* It is a bad symptom that Chœrilus should complain, in the first verses of his poem, that the subjects of epic poetry were already exhausted: † this could not have been his motive if he had undertaken to paint the greatest deed of the Greeks. But, in general, a striving after *novelty* seems to have produced marked effects upon his works, both in general and in the details. Aristotle finds fault with his comparisons as far-fetched and obscure; ‡ and even the fragments have been sometimes justly censured for their forced and artificial tone. §

The *Thebais* of ANTIMACHUS was formed on a wide and comprehensive plan; there was mythological lore in the execution of the details, and careful study in the choice of expressions; but the whole poem was deficient, according to the judgment of the ancient critics, in that natural connexion which arrests and detains the attention, and in that charm of poetic feeling which no laborious industry or elaborate refinement can produce. ‖ Hadrian, therefore, remained true to his predilection for everything showy, affected, and unnatural, when he placed Antimachus before Homer, and attempted an epic imitation of the style of the former. ¶

---

* It is clear that the Athenians did not pay Chœrilus a golden stater for every verse, as has been inferred from Suidas: it is obvious that this is a confusion with the later Chœrilus, whom Alexander rewarded in so princely a manner. Horat. *Ep.* II. 1, 233.

† Ἆ μάκαρ ὅστις ἔην κεῖνον χρόνον ἴδρις ἀοιδῶν
Μουσάων θεράπων, ὅτ' ἀκήρατος ἦν ἔτι λειμών.
νῦν δ' ὅτε πάντα δέδασται, ἔχουσι δὲ πείρατα τέχναι,
ὕστατοι αὖτε δρόμου καταλειπόμεθ'· οὐδέ πη ἔστιν
πάντη παπταίνοντα νεοζυγὲς ἅρμα πελάσσαι.

These verses are preserved in the Scholiast to Aristot. Rhet. III. 14, § 4, in Gaisford's *Animadversiones* (Oxon. 1820). Compare Naeke's *Chœrilus*, p. 104.

‡ Aristot. *Topic.* VIII. 1.

§ A. F. Naeke, *Chœrili Samii quæ supersunt. Lips.* 1817.

‖ *Antimachi Colophonii reliquiæ,* ed. Schellenberg, p. 38, seq.

¶ Spartianus in the life of Hadrian, c. 15. The title of Hadrian's work is now known to have been *Catachanæ;* the poem probably had some resemblance to the *Catonis Diræ* of Valerius.

CHAPTER XXXI.

§ 1. Importance of prose at this period. § 2. Oratory at Athens rendered necessary by the democratical form of government. § 3. Themistocles; Pericles: power of their oratory. § 4. Characteristics of their oratory in relation to their opinions and modes of thought. § 5. Form and style of their speeches.

§ 1. WE have seen both tragedy and comedy in their latter days gradually sinking into prose; and this has shown us that prose was the most powerful instrument in the literature of the time, and has made us the more curious to investigate its tendency, its progress, and its developement.

The cultivation of prose belongs almost entirely to the period which intervened between the Persian war and the time of Alexander the Great. Before this time every attempt at prose composition was either so little removed from the colloquial style of the day, as to forfeit all claim to be considered as a written language, properly so called: or else owed all its charms and splendour to an imitation of the diction and the forms of words found in poetry, which attained to completeness and maturity many hundred years before the rise of a prose literature.

In considering the history of Attic prose, we propose to give a view of the general character of the works of the prose writers, and· their relation to the circumstances of the Athenian people, to their intellectual energy and elasticity, and to the mixture of reason and passion which was so conspicuous among them. But it is obvious that it will not be possible to do this without carefully examining the contents, the subjects, and the practical and theoretical objects of these works.

We may distinguish three epochs in the general history of Attic prose, from Pericles to Alexander the Great: the first that of Pericles himself, Antiphon, and Thucydides; the second, that of Lysias, Isocrates, and Plato; the third, that of Demosthenes, Æschines, and Demades. The sequel will show why we have selected these names.

Two widely different causes co-operated in introducing the first epoch: —*Athenian politics* and *Sicilian sophistry*. We must first take a view of these two causes.

§ 2. Since the time of Solon, the most distinguished statesmen of Athens had formed some general views with regard to the destination of their native city, based upon a profound consideration of the external relations and internal resources of Attica, and the peculiar capabilities of the inhabitants. An extension of the democracy, industry, and trade, and, above all, the sovereignty of the sea, were the primary objects which those statesmen proposed to themselves. Some peculiar views

were transmitted through a series of statesmen,* from Solon to Themistocles and Pericles, and were from time to time further developed and
extended; and though an opposite party in politics (that of Aristides and
Cimon) endeavoured to set bounds to this developement, the point for
which they contended did not affect any one of the leading principles
which guided the other party; they only wished to moderate the sudden-
ness and violence of the movement.

This deep reflection on and clear perception of what was needful for
Athens,† imparted to the speeches of men like Themistocles and Pericles
a power and solidity which made a far deeper impression on the people
of Athens than any particular proposal or counsel could have done.
Public speaking had been common in Greece from the earliest times;
long before popular assemblies had gained the sovereign power by the
establishment of democracy, the ancient kings had been in the habit
of addressing their people, sometimes with that natural eloquence which
Homer ascribes to Ulysses, at other times, like Menelaus, with concise
but persuasive diction: · Hesiod assigns to kings a muse of their own,—
Calliope—by whose aid they were enabled to speak convincingly and
persuasively in the popular assembly and from the seat of judgment.
With the further developement of republican constitutions after the age
of Homer and Hesiod, public officers and demagogues without number
had spoken in the public meetings, or in the deliberative councils and
legislative committees of the numerous independent states, and no doubt
they often spoke eloquently and wisely; but these speeches did not survive the particular occasion which called them forth: they were wasted
on the air without leaving behind them a more lasting effect than would
have been produced by a discourse of common life; and in this whole
period it seems never to have been imagined that oratory could produce
effects more lasting than the particular occurrence which gave occasion
for a display of it, or that it was capable of exerting a ruling influence
over all the actions and inclinations of a people. Even the lively and
ingenious Ionians were distinguished at the flourishing epoch of their
literature, for an amusing style, adapted to such narratives as might be
communicated in private society, rather than for the more powerful
eloquence of the public assembly: at least Herodotus, whose history may
be considered as belonging to Ionian literature, though he is fond of
introducing dialogues and short speeches, never incorporates with his
history the popular harangues which are so remarkable in Thucy-

* See Plutarch, *Themist.* 2. Themistocles studied as a young man under Mne-
siphilus, who makes such a distinguished appearance in Herod. VIII. 57, and
who had devoted himself to the so called σοφία, which, according to Plutarch,
consisted in political capacity and practical understanding, and which had descended
from Solon.

† Τοῦ δέοντος, an expression which was very common at Athens in the time of
Pericles, and denoted whatever was expedient under the existing circumstances
of the state.

dides. It is unanimously agreed among the ancients that Athens was
the native soil of oratory,* and as the works of Athenian orators alone
have come down to us, so also we may safely conclude that the ruder
oratory, not designed for literary preservation, but from which oratory,
as a branch of literature, arose, was cultivated in a much higher degree
among the Athenians than in all the rest of Greece.

§ 3. THEMISTOCLES, who with equal courage and genius had laid the
foundations of the greatness of Athens at the most dangerous and difficult
crisis of her history, was not distinguished for eloquence, so much as
for the wisdom of his plans, and the energy with which he carried them
out; nevertheless, it is universally agreed that he was in the highest
degree capable of unfolding his views, and of recommending them by
argument.† The oratory of *Pericles* occupies a much more prominent
position. The power and dominion of Athens, though continually assailed
by new enemies, seemed at last to have acquired some stability: it was
time to survey the advantages which had been gained, and to become
acquainted with the principles which had led 'to their acquisition and
might contribute to their increase : the question too arose, what use should
be made of this dominion over the Greeks of the islands and the 'coasts,
which it had cost so much trouble to obtain, and of the revenues which
flowed into Athens in such abundant streams. It is manifest, from the
whole political career of Pericles, that on the one hand he presupposed
in his people a power of governing themselves, and on the other hand
that he wished to prevent the state from becoming a mere stake to
be played for by ambitious demagogues : for he favoured every institu-
tion which gave the poorer citizens a share in the government; he
encouraged everything which might contribute to extend education and
knowledge; and by his astonishing expenditure on works of architec-
ture and sculpture, he gave the people a decided fondness for the grand
and beautiful. And thus the appearance of Pericles on the bema (which
he purposely reserved for great occasions‡) was not intended merely
to aid the passing of some law, but was at the same time calculated
to infuse a noble spirit into the general politics of Athens, to guide
the views of the Athenians in regard to their external relations and all
the difficulties of their position; and it was the wish of this true friend
of the people that all this might long survive himself. This is obviously
the opinion of Thucydides, whom we may consider as in many respects a
worthy disciple of the school of Pericles ; and this is the representation
which he has given us of the oratory of that statesman in the three
speeches (all of them delivered on important occasions) which he has

---

* *Studium eloquentiæ proprium Athenarum*, Cicero, *Brutus*, XIII.
    † Not to mention other authorities, Lysias (*Epitaph.* XLII.) says that he was
'Ικανώτατος εἰπεῖν καὶ γνῶναι καὶ πρᾶξαι.
    ‡ Plutarch, *Pericles* VII.

put into his mouth. This wonderful triad of speeches forms a beautiful whole, which is perfect and complete in itself. The *first* speech[*] proves the necessity of a war with the Peloponnesians, and the probability that it will be successful: the *second*,[†] delivered immediately after the first successes obtained in the war, under the form of a funeral oration, confirms the Athenians in their mode of living and acting; it is half an apology for, half a panegyric upon Athens: it is full of a sense of truth and of noble self-reliance, tempered with moderation; the *third*,[‡] delivered after the calamities which had befallen Athens, rather through the plague than through the war, and which had nevertheless made the people vacillate in their resolutions, offers the consolation most worthy of a noble heart, namely, that up to that time fortune, on which no man can count, had deceived them, but they had not been misled by their own calculations and convictions; and that these would never deceive them if they did not allow themselves to be led astray by some unforeseen accidents.[§]

§ 4. No speech of Pericles has been preserved in writing. It may seem surprising that no attempt was made to write down and preserve, for the benefit of the present and future generations, works which every one considered admirable, and which were regarded as, in some respects, the most perfect specimens of oratory.[||] The only explanation of this that can be offered is, that in those days a speech was not considered as possessing any value or interest, save in reference to the particular practical object for which it was designed: it had never occurred to people that speeches and poems might be placed in one class, and both preserved, without reference to their subjects, on account of the skill with which the subjects were treated, and the general beauties of the form and composition.[¶] Only a few emphatic and nervous expressions of Pericles were kept in remembrance; but a general impression of the grandeur and copiousness of his oratory long prevailed among the Greeks. We are enabled, partly by this long prevalent impression, which is mentioned even by later writers, and partly by the connexion between Pericles and the other old Attic orators, as also with Thucydides, to form a clear conception of his style of speaking, without drawing much upon our imagination.

* Thucyd. I., 140—144.   † Thucyd. II. 35—46.   ‡ Thucyd. II. 60—64.

§ A speech of Pericles, in which he took a general survey of the military power and resources of Athens, is given by Thucydides (II. 13,) indirectly and in outline, because this was not an opportunity for unfolding a train of leading ideas.

|| Plato, though not very partial to Pericles, nevertheless considers him as τελειότατος εἰς τὴν ῥητορικήν, and refers for the cause to his acquaintance with the speculations of Anaxagoras, *Phædr.* 270. Cicero, in his *Brutus* XII., calls him "oratorem *prope* perfectum," only to leave something to be said for the other orators.

¶ [All the speeches which have been preserved to us from antiquity have been preserved by the orators themselves. Pericles appears to have made no record of his speeches; and probably he would have considered it degrading, in his eminent position, to place himself on the footing of a λογογράφος.—*Editor.*]

The primary characteristic of the oratory of Pericles, and those who most resembled him is, that their speeches are full of thoughts concisely expressed. Unaccustomed to continued abstraction, and unwilling to indulge in trivial reasonings, their powers of reflection seized on all the circumstances of the world around them with fresh and unimpaired vigour, and, assisted by abundant experience and acute observations, brought the light of their clear general conceptions to bear upon every subject which they took up. Cicero characterizes Pericles, Alcibiades, and Thucydides, (for he rightly reckons the two latter among the orators,) by the epithets " subtle, acute, and concise,"[*] and distinguishes between them and the somewhat younger generation of Critias, Theramenes, and Lysias, who had also, he says, retained some of the sap and life-blood of Pericles,[†] but had spun the thread of their discourse rather more liberally.[‡]

With regard to the opinions of Pericles, we know that they were remarkable for the comprehensive views of public affairs on which they were based. The majesty for which Pericles was so distinguished, and which gained for him the appellation of " the Olympian," consisted mostly in the skill and ability with which he referred all common occurrences to the general principles and bold ideas, which he had derived from his noble and exalted view of the destiny of Athens. Accordingly, Plato says of Pericles, that in addition to his natural abilities, he had acquired an elevation of mind and a habit of striving after definite objects.[§] It was on this account, too, that his opinions took such a firm hold of his hearers ; according to the metaphor of Eupolis—they remained fixed in the mind, like the sting of the bee.

§ 5. It was because the thoughts of Pericles were so striking, so entirely to the purpose, and at the same time so grand, and we may add it was on this account *alone*, that his speeches produced so deep and lasting an impression. The sole object of the oratory of Pericles was to produce conviction, to give a permanent bias to the mind of the people. It was alien from his intentions to excite any sudden and transient burst of passion by working on the emotions of the heart. The whole history of Attic oratory teaches us that there could not be in the

[*] He says *subtiles, acuti, breves, sententiis magis quam verbis abundantes*, by which he means, " skilful in the choice of words, and in the distinct expression of every thought" (*subtiles*), " refined in their ideas" (*acuti*), " concise" (*breves*), " and with more thoughts than words."

[†] *Retinebant illum Periclis succum.*

[‡] *De Orator.* II. 22. In the *Brutus*, c. VII., he gives a rather different classification of the old orators. In the latter work he classes Alcibiades along with Critias and Theramenes, and says the style of their oratory may be gathered from Thucydides ; he calls them *grandes verbis, crebri sententiis, compressione rerum breves, et ob eam causam subobscuri*. Critias is described by Philostratus, *Sophist.* I. 16, and still better by Hermogenes, περὶ ἰδῶν, (in Walz, *Rhet. Græci.* L. III., p. 388) : and we may infer that he stood, in regard to style, between Antiphon and Lysias.

[§] Plato, *Phædrus*, p. 270 : τὸ ὑψηλόνουν τοῦτο καὶ πάντῃ τελεσιουργὸν . . . ὁ Περικλῆς πρὸς τὸ εὐφυὴς εἶναι ἐκτήσατο. The τελεσιουργὸν denotes, according to the context, the striving after a great fixed object.

speeches of Pericles the slightest employment of those means by which the orators of a later age used to set in motion the violent and unruly impulses of the multitude. To judge from the descriptions which have been given of the manner of Pericles when he ascended the bema, it was tranquil, with hardly any change of feature, with calm and dignified gestures ; his garments were. undisturbed by oratorical gesticulations of any kind, and the tone and loudness of his voice were equable and sustained.* We may conceive that the frame of mind which this delivery expressed, and which it excited in the hearers, was in harmony and unison with it. Pericles had no wish to gratify the people otherwise than by ministering to their improvement and benefit. He never condescended to flatter them. Great as was his idea of the resources and high destinies of Athens, he never feared in particular cases to tell them even the harshest truths. When Pericles declaimed against the people, this was thought, according to Cicero, a proof of his affection towards them, and produced a pleasing impression ;† even when his own safety was threatened, he was content to wait till they had an opportunity of becoming convinced of his innocence, and he never sought to produce this conviction otherwise than by a clear and energetic representation of the truth, studiously avoiding any appeal to transient emotions and feelings. He was just as little anxious to amuse or entertain the populace. Pericles never indulged in a smile while speaking from the bema.‡ His dignity never stooped to merriment.§ All his public appearances were marked by a sustained earnestness of manner.

Some traditional particulars and the character of the time enable us also to form an opinion of the diction of the speeches of Pericles. He employed the language of common life, the vernacular idiom of Attica, even more than Thucydides :‖ but his accurate discrimination of meanings gave his words a subtilty and pregnancy which was a main ingredient in the nervous energy of his style. Although there was more of reasoning than of imagination in his speeches, he had no difficulty in giving a vivid and impressive colouring to his language by the use of striking metaphors and comparisons, and as the prose of the day was altogether unformed, by so doing, he could not help expressing himself poetically. A good many of these figurative expressions and apophthegms in the speeches of Pericles have been preserved, and especially by Aristotle : as when he said of the Samians, that " they were like little children who cried when they took their food ;" or when at the funeral of a number of young persons who had fallen in battle, he used the beautiful figure, that " the year had lost its spring."¶

* Plutarch. *Pericl.* V.
† Cicero, *de Orat.* III. 34.
‡ Plutarch, *Pericl.* 5: προσώπου σύστασις ἄθρυπτος εἰς γίλωτα.
§ *Summa auctoritas sine omni hilaritate,* Cic. *de Offic.* I. 30.
‖ This appears from the fact mentioned near the end of Chap. XXVII.
¶ Aristotle, *Rhetor.* I. 7 ; III. 4, 10.

CHAPTER XXXII.

§ 1. Profession of the Sophists: essential elements of their doctrines. The principles of Protagoras. § 2. Opinions of Gorgias. Pernicious effects of his doctrines, especially as they were carried out by his disciples. § 3. Important services of the Sophists in forming a prose style: different tendencies of the Sicilian and other Sophists in this respect. § 4. The rhetoric of Gorgias. § 5. His forms of expression.

§ 1. THE impulse to a further improvement of the prose style proceeded immediately from the Sophists, who, in general, exercised a greater influence on the culture of the Greek mind than any other class of men, the ancient poets alone excepted.

The Sophists were, as their name indicates, persons who made knowledge their profession, and who undertook to impart it to every one who was willing to place himself under their guidance. The philosophers of the Socratic school reproached them with being the first to sell knowledge for money; and such was the case; for they not only demanded admittance-money from those who came to hear their public lectures (ἐπιδείξεις),* but also undertook for a considerable sum, fixed before-hand, to give young men a complete sophistical education, and not to dismiss them till they were thoroughly instructed in their art. At that time a thirst for knowledge was so great in Greece,† that not only in Athens, but also in the oligarchies of Thessaly, hearers and pupils flocked to them in crowds; the arrival in any city of one of the greater sophists, Gorgias, Protagoras, or Hippias, was celebrated as a festival; and these men acquired riches such as art and science had never before earned among the Greeks.

Not only the outward profession, but also the peculiar doctrines of the Sophists were, on the whole, one and the same, though they admitted of certain modifications of greater or less importance. If we consider these doctrines philosophically, they amounted to *a denial or renunciation of all true science*. Philosophy had then just completed the first stage of her career: she had boldly undertaken to solve the abstrusest questions of speculation, and the widely different answers which had been returned to some of those questions, had all produced conviction and obtained many staunch supporters. The difference between the results thus obtained, although the grounds of this difference had not been investigated, must of itself have awakened a doubt as to the possibility of any real

* There were wide differences in the amounts paid on these occasions. The admission-fee for some lectures was a drachma, for others fifty drachmæ.
† Comp. the remark in Chap. XXVII., § 5.

knowledge regarding the hidden nature of things. Accordingly, nothing was more likely than that every flight of speculation should be succeeded by an epoch of scepticism, in which the universality of all science would be doubted or denied. That all knowledge is *subjective*, that it is true only for the individual, was the meaning of the celebrated saying * of . PROTAGORAS OF ABDERA, who made his appearance at Athens in the time of Pericles,† and for a long time enjoyed a great reputation there, till at last a reaction was caused by the bold scepticism of his opinions, and he was banished from Athens and his books were publicly burnt.‡ Agreeing with Heraclitus in regard to the doctrine of a perpetual motion and of a continual change in the impressions and perceptions of men, he deduced from this that the individual could know nothing beyond these ever varying perceptions ; consequently, that whatever *appeared to be, was so* for the individual. According to this doctrine, opposite opinions on the same subject might be equally true ; and if an opinion were only supported by a momentary appearance of truth, this was sufficient to make it true for the moment. Hence, it was one of the great feats which Protagoras and the other Sophists professed to perform, to be able to speak with equal plausibility *for* and *against* the same position ; not in order to discover the truth, but in order to show the nothingness of truth. It was not, however, the intention of Protágoras to deprive virtue, as well as truth, of its reality : but he reduced virtue to a mere state or condition of the subject,—a set of impressions and feelings which rendered the subject more capable of active usefulness. Of the gods, he said at the very beginning of the book which caused his banishment from Athens : " With regard to the gods, I cannot determine whether they are or are not ; for there are many obstacles in the way of this inquiry—the uncertainty of the matter, and the shortness of human life."

§ 2. GORGIAS, of Leontini, in Sicily, who visited Athens for the first time in Ol. 88, 2. B.C. 427, as an ambassador from his native town, belonged to an entirely different part of the Hellenic world, had different teachers, and proceeded from an older philosophical school than Protagoras, but yet there was a great correspondence between the pursuits of these two men ; and from this we may clearly see how strongly the spirit of the age must have inclined to the form and mode of speculation which was common to them both. Gorgias employed the dialectical method of the Eleatic school, but arrived at an opposite result by means of it : while the Eleatic philosophers directed all their efforts towards establishing the perpetuity and unity of existence, Gorgias availed

---

* Πάντων μέτρον ἄνθρωπος.

† About Ol. 84. B.C. 444, according to the chronology of Apollodorus.

‡ Protagoras was prosecuted for atheism and expelled from Athens, on the accusation of Pythodorus, one of the council of the Four-hundred : this would be in Ol. 92, 1. or 2. B.C. 411, if the event happened during the time of the Four-hundred, but this is by no means established.

to democratic sentiments (Ol. 78, 3. B.C. 466), and by the complicated transactions which sprung up from the renewal of private claims long suppressed by the tyrants.* At this time CORAX, who had been highly esteemed by the tyrant Hiero, came forward in a conspicuous manner, both as a public orator and as a pleader in the law-courts ; † his great practice led him to consider more accurately the principles of his art ; and at last it occurred to him to write a book on the subject ;‡ this book, like the innumerable treatises which succeeded it, was called τέχνη ῥητορική, " the art of rhetoric," or simply τέχνη, " the art." Although this work might have been very circumscribed in its plan, and not very comprehensive in its treatment of the subject, it is nevertheless worthy of notice as the first of its kind, not only among the Greeks, but perhaps also in the whole world. For this τέχνη of Corax was not merely the first attempt at a theory of rhetoric, but also the first theoretical book on any branch of art ; § and it is highly remarkable that while ancient poetry was transmitted through so many generations by nothing but practice and oral instruction, its younger sister began at once with establishing itself in the form of a theory, and as such communicating itself to all who were desirous of learning its principles. All that we know of this τέχνη is that it laid down a regular form and regular divisions for the oration ; above all, it was to begin with a distinct procemium, calculated to put the hearers in a favourable train, and to conciliate their good will at the very opening of the speech. ‖

§ 4. TISIAS was first a pupil and afterwards a rival of Corax ; he was also known not only as an orator, but also as the author of a τέχνη. Gorgias, again, was the pupil of Tisias, and followed closely in his steps : according to one account,¶ Tisias was a colleague of Gorgias in the embassy from Leontini mentioned above, though the pupil was at that time infinitely more celebrated than his master. With Gorgias this artificial rhetoric obtained more fame and glory than fell to the share

---

* Cic., *Brut.* XII., 46 (after Aristotle): *cum sublatis in Sicilia tyrannis res privatæ longo intervallo judiciis repeterentur.* Aristotle is also the authority for the statement in the scholia on Hermogenes, in Reiske's *Oratores Attici.* T. VIII. p. 196. Comp. Montfaucon, *Biblioth. Coislin.*, p. 592.

† Or as a composer of speeches for others, for it is doubtful whether there was an establishment of *patroni* and *causidici* at Syracuse, as at Rome; or whether every one was compelled to plead his own cause, as at Athens, in which case he was always able to get his speech made for him by some professed rhetorician.

‡ This is also mentioned by Aristotle, who wrote a history of rhetoric down to his own time, which is now lost : besides the passages referred to above, he mentions the τέχνη of Corax in his *Rhetor.* II., 24.

§ The old architectural treatises on particular buildings, such as that of Theodorus of Samos on the temple of Juno in that island, and those of Chersiphron and Metagenes on the temple of Diana at Ephesus, were probably only tables of calculations and measurements.

‖ These introductions were called κολακευτικὰ καὶ θεραπευτικὰ προοίμια.

¶ See Pausan. VI., 17, 18. Diodorus, the principal authority, makes no mention of Tisias, XI., 53.

of any other branch of literature. The Athenians, to whom this Sicilian rhetoric was still a novelty, though they were fully qualified and predisposed to appreciate and enjoy its beauties,* were quite enchanted with it, and it soon became fashionable to speak like Gorgias. The impression produced by the oratory of Gorgias was greatly increased by his stately appearance, his well-chosen and splendid costume, and the self-possession and confidence of his demeanour. Besides, his rhetoric rested on a basis of philosophy,† though, as has just been mentioned, rather of a negative kind; and there is no trace of this in the systems of Corax and Tisias. This philosophy taught, that the sole aim of the orator is to turn the minds of his hearers into such a train as may best consist with his own interests; that, consequently, rhetoric is the agent of persuasion,‡ the art of all arts, because the rhetorician is able to speak well and convincingly on every subject, even though he has no accurate knowledge respecting it.

In accordance with this view of rhetoric, Gorgias took little pains with the subject-matter of his speeches; he only concerned himself about this so far as to exercise himself in treating of general topics, which were called *loci communes*, and the proper management and application of which have always helped the rhetorician to conceal his ignorance. The panegyrics and invectives which Gorgias wrote on every possible subject, and which served him for practice, were also calculated to assist him in combating or defending received opinions and convictions, by palliating the bad, and misrepresenting the good. The same purpose was served by his delusive and captious conclusions, which he had borrowed from the Eleatic school, in order to pass with the common herd as a profound thinker, and to confuse their notions of truth and falsehood. All this belonged to the instrument, by virtue of which Gorgias promised, in the language of the day, to make the *weaker argument, i. e.* the worse cause, victorious over the *stronger argument, i. e.* the better cause.§

§ 5. But the chief study of Gorgias was directed to the form of expression; and it is true that he was able, by the use of high-sounding words and artfully constructed sentences, to deceive not only the ears but also the mind of the Greeks—alive as they were to the perception of such beauties—to so great an extent that they overlooked for a long time the emptiness and coldness of his declamations. Prose was at this time commencing its career, and had not yet manifested its resources, and shown the beauty of which it was capable: it was natural, therefore,

* ὅστις εὐφυῶς καὶ φιλολόγοι, says Diodorus.
† This philosophy is contained in a treatise by Gorgias, περὶ φύσεως ἢ τοῦ μὴ ὄντος, of which the best account is given by Aristotle in his essay on Melissus, Xenophanes, and Gorgias.
‡ Πειθοῦς δημιουργός.   § ἥττων καὶ κρείττων λόγος.

speaking,* there was yet no one man in Athens who was better able to
assist, by his counsels, those who had any contest to undergo either in the
law-courts 'or in the popular assemblies. And in his own case, when,
after the downfal of the Four-hundred, he was tried for his life as having
been a party to the establishment of the oligarchy, it is acknowledged
that the speech which he made in his own defence was the best that had
ever been made up to that time." † But his admirable oratory was of
no avail at this crisis, when the effect of his speech was more than counter-
balanced by the feelings of the people: the devices of Theramenes
completed his ruin; he was executed in Ol. 92, 2. B.C. 411, when
nearly seventy years old; ‡ his property was confiscated, and even his
descendants were deprived of the rights of citizenship. §

We clearly see, from the testimony of Thucydides, what use Antiphon
made of his oratory. He did not come forward, like other speakers, to
express his sentiments in the *Ecclesia,* nor was he ever a public accuser
in the law-courts: he never spoke in public save on his own affairs and
when attacked: in other cases he laboured for others. With him the
business of *speech-writing* first rose into importance, a business which
for a long time was not considered so honourable as that of the public
speaker; but although many Athenians spoke and thought contemptuously of this profession, it was practised even by the great public orators
along with their other employments; and according to the Athenian
institutions was almost indispensable. For in private suits the parties
themselves pleaded their cause in open court; and in public indictments,
though any Athenian might conduct the prosecution, the accused person
was not allowed an advocate, though his defence might be supported by
some friends who spoke after him, and endeavoured to complete the
arguments in his favour. It is obvious from this, that when the need
of an advocate in the law-courts began to be more and more felt, most
Athenians would be obliged to apply for professional assistance, and
would, with this view, either get assisted in the composition of their
own speeches, or commit to memory and deliver, word for word, a speech
composed for them by some practised orator. Thus the speech-writers,
or *logographi,* as they were called, ‖ (Antiphon, Lysias, Isæus, and
Demosthenes,) rendered services partly analogous to those performed by
the Roman *patroni* and *causidici,* or to the legal advocates and coun-

* διανότης, here used in its wider sense, as implying any power of persuasion.
† It is a great pity that this speech has not been preserved. Harpocration often
quotes it under the title ἐν τῷ περὶ τῆς μεταστάσεως. The allusions to the time of
the Four-hundred are obvious enough.
‡ i. e. if the account is true which places his birth in Ol. 75, 1. B.C. 480. His
great age and winning eloquence seem to have gained him the name of *Nestor,* by
which he was known among the Athenian people.
§ The decree according to which he was executed, and the decision of the court,
are preserved in the *Vitæ decem oratorum* (in Plutarch's works), Cap. I.
‖ They were called λογογράφοι by the common people at Athens.

sellors of modern states, although they did not stand nearly so high in public estimation, unless at the same time they took an active part in public affairs.* The practice of writing speeches for others probably led to a general habit of committing speeches to writing, and thus placing them within the reach of others besides those to whom they were delivered : at all events, it is certain that Antiphon was the first to do this. †

Antiphon also established a *school* of rhetoric, in which the art of oratory was systematically taught, and, according to a custom which had been prevalent since the time of Corax, wrote a *Techne*, containing a formal exposition of his principles. As a teacher of rhetoric, Antiphon followed closely in the steps of the Sophists, with whose works he was very well acquainted, although he was not actually a scholar of any one among them : ‡ like Protagoras and Gorgias, he discussed general themes, which were designed only for exercises, and had no practical object in view. These may have been partly the most general subjects about which an argument could be held,—the *loci communes*, as they are called ; § partly, particular cases so ingeniously contrived that the contrary assertions respecting them might be maintained with equal facility, and thus exercise would be afforded to the sophistic art of speaking plausibly on both sides of the question.

§ 2. Of the fifteen remaining speeches of Antiphon, twelve belong to the class of school exercises. They form three *Tetralogies*, so that every four of the orations are occupied with the discussion of the same case, and contain a speech and reply by both plaintiff and defendant. ‖ The following is the subject of the first Tetralogy :—A citizen, returning with his slave from an evening banquet, is attacked by assassins, and killed on the spot : the slave is mortally wounded, but survives till he has told the relations of the murdered man that he recognized among the assassins a particular person who was at enmity with his master, and who was about to lose his cause in an important law-suit between him and the deceased. Accordingly, this person is indicted by the family of the murdered man, and the speeches all turn upon an attempt to exaggerate or diminish the probabilities for and against the guilt of the person arraigned. For instance, while the complainant lays the greatest stress on the animosity

* Thus Antiphon was attacked by Plato the comedian for writing speeches for hire : Photius, *Codex* 259.
† *Orationem primus omnium scripsit*, says Quintilian.
‡ This is shown by the γίνος Ἀντιφῶντος : the chronology renders it almost impossible that Antiphon's father could have been a Sophist (*Vitæ* X. *Orat.*, c. 1. Phot., *Codex* 259).—[This is probably a confusion occasioned by the name of Antiphon's father *Sophilus*.—Ed.]
§ That Antiphon had practised himself in such common places is shown by their occurrence in different orations, in which he inserts them wherever he can. Comp. *de cæde Herod.*, § 14, 87. *Chor.*, § 2, 3.
‖ λόγοι πρότεροι καὶ ὕστεροι.

VOL. II.   G

existing between the accused and the deceased, the defendant maintains
that he could certainly have had no hand in the murder, when it was
obvious that the first suspicion would fall on himself.   While the former
sets great value on the evidence of the slave as the only one available for
his purpose, the latter maintains that slaves would not be tortured as they
were, according to the Greek custom, unless their simple testimony had
been considered insufficient.   In answer to this the complainant urges,
in his second speech, that slaves were tortured on account of theft, for
the purpose of bringing to light some transgression which they concealed
to please their master ; but that, in cases like the one in question, they
were emancipated in order that they might be qualified to give evidence ;*
and, in regard to the argument that the accused must have foreseen that he
would be suspected, the fear of this suspicion would not have been sufficient to counterbalance the danger resulting from the loss of his cause.
The accused, however, gives a turn to the argument from probability,
by remarking, among other things, that a freeman would be restrained
from giving a false testimony by a fear of endangering his reputation and
substance ; but that there was nothing to hinder the slave at the point
of death from gratifying the family of his master, by impeaching his
master's old enemy.   And after having compared all the arguments
from probability, and drawn a balance in his own favour, he concludes
aptly enough, by saying that he can prove his innocence not merely by
probabilities † but by facts, and accordingly offers all his slaves, male and
female, to be tortured according to the custom of Athens, in order to
prove that he never left his house on the night of the murder.

We have selected these few points from many other arguments equally
acute on both sides of the question, in order to give those readers who are
not yet acquainted with Antiphon's speeches, some notion, however faint,
of the shrewdness and ingenuity with which the rhetoricians of that time
could twist and turn to their own purposes the facts and circumstances
which they were called upon to discuss.   The sophistic art of strength-
ening the weaker cause was in Antiphon's school connected with forensic
oratory, ‡ the professor of which must necessarily be prepared to argue
in favour of either of the parties in a law-suit.

§ 3. Besides these rhetorical exercises, we have three of Antiphon's
speeches which were actually delivered in court—the accusation of a
step mother charged with poisoning, the defence of the person charged
with the murder of Herodes, and another defence of a choregus, one

* Personal freedom was indispensable for evidence (μαρτυρεῖν) properly so called :
slaves were compelled to give evidence by the torture.
† In § 10, he says with great acuteness : " While they maintain on grounds of
probability that I am guilty, they nevertheless maintain that I am not *probably* but
actually the murderer."
‡ τὸ δικανικὸν γένος.

of whose choreutæ had been poisoned while under training. All these speeches refer to charges of murder,* and for this reason have been classed with the Tetralogies, the assumed subjects of which are of the same kind : a distribution of the works of Greek orators according to the nature of the different suits was very common among the learned grammarians,† and many ancient citations refer to this division ; for instance, when speeches referring to the duties of guardians, to money-transactions, or to debts, are quoted as belonging to different classes. In this manner Antiphon's speeches on charges of murder have alone been preserved, and the only orations of Isæus which have come down to us, are those on the law of inheritance and wills. In these speeches of Antiphon we see the same ingenuity and shrewdness, and the same legal acumen, as in the Tetralogies, combined with far greater polish and elaboration of style, since the Tetralogies were only designed to display skill in the discovery and complication of arguments.

These more complete speeches may be reckoned among the most important materials that we possess for a history of oratory. In respect to their style, they stand in close connexion with the history of Thucydides and the speeches with which it is interspersed, and confirm the statement of many grammarians, ‡ that Thucydides was instructed in the school of Antiphon,—a statement which harmonizes very well with the circumstances of their lives. The ancients often couple Thucydides with Antiphon, § and mention these two as the chief masters of the old austere oratory, ‖ the nature of which we must here endeavour rightly to comprehend. It does not consist (as might be conjectured from the expressions used in speaking of it,¶ which are justified only by a comparison with the smooth and polished oratory of later days) in any intentional rudeness or harshness, but in the orator's confining himself to a clear and definite expression of what he had clearly and definitely conceived. Although it is not to be denied that the orators of that time were deficient in the fluency which results from practice, they had on that account all the more power and freshness of thought ; many reflections, which afterwards became trivial from frequent repetition, and in this way came to be used in a flippant and superficial manner, were then delivered with all the energetic earnestness of real feeling ; and, without taking into

---

* φονικαὶ δίκαι.   † This occurs frequently in Dionysius of Halicarnassus.
‡ The most important authority is Cæcilius of Calacte, a distinguished rhetorician of Cicero's time, many of whose striking judgments and important remarks are still extant. See the *Vitæ* X. *Orator.*, c. 1. Photius, *Biblioth. Codex*, 259.
§ When rhetorical studies were still a novelty, Thucydides at the age of twenty might easily have been the scholar of Antiphon, who was eight years his senior.
‖ Dionys. Hal., *de verb. comp.*, p. 150, Reiske. Tryphon, in Walz, *Rhet.*, t. VIII., p. 750.
¶ αὐστηρὸς χαρακτήρ, αὐστηρὰ ἁρμονία, *austerum dicendi genus* ; see Dionys. Hal., *de compos. verborum*, p. 147, seqq.

consideration the value and importance of their works as products of
human genius, we find in writers like Antiphon and Thucydides a continual liveliness, an inexhaustible vigour of mind, which, not to go
farther, places them above even Plato and Demosthenes, notwithstanding
their better training and wider experience.

§ 4. We shall arrive at a clearer conception of the train of thought in
these writers by considering, first the words, and then the syntactical
combinations by which their style was distinguished. Great accuracy in
the use of expressions* is a characteristic as well of Antiphon as of
Thucydides. This is manifested, among other things, by an attempt to
make a marked distinction between synonyms and words of similar
sound: this originated with Prodicus, and both in this Sophist and in the
authors of whom we are speaking occasionally gave an air of extravagance and affectation to their style.† Not to speak of individual words,
the luxuriance of grammatical forms in the Greek language and the
readiness with which it admitted new compounds, enabled these authors
to create whole classes of expressions indicating the most delicate shades
of meaning, such as the neuter participles.‡ In regard to the grammatical forms and the connecting particles, the old writers did not
strive after that regular continuity which gives an equable flow to the
discourse, and enables one to see the whole connexion from any part
of it: they considered it of more importance to express the finer modifications of meaning by changes in the form of words, even though this
might produce abruptness and difficulty in the expressions. § With
respect to the connexion of the sentences with one another, the language of Antiphon and Thucydides stands half-way between the consecutive but unconnected diction of Herodotus‖ and the periodic
style of the school of Isocrates. We shall consider in one of the
following chapters how the period, which conveys an idea of a style
finished and rounded off, was first cultivated in that later school: here
it will be sufficient to mention the total want of such a finished periodic
completeness in the writings of Antiphon and Thucydides. There

* ἀκριβολογία ἐπὶ τοῖς ὀνόμασιν, Marcellin., vita Thucyd., § 36.

† As when Antiphon says (de caed. Herod., § 94, according to the probable reading): "You are now scrutineers (γνωρισταί) of the evidence; then you will be
judges (δικασταί) of the suit: you are now only guessers (δοξασταί), you will then
be deciders (κριταί) of the truth." See the similar examples in §§ 91, 92.

‡ As when Antiphon says (Tetral. I., γ. § 3): "The danger and the disgrace,
which had greater influence than the quarrel, were sufficient to subdue the passion
that was boiling in his mind" (σωφρονίσαι τὸ θυμούμενον τῆς γνώμης). Thucydides,
who is as partial as Antiphon to this mode of expression, also uses the phrase,
τὸ θυμούμενον τῆς γνώμης, VIII. 68.

§ As an example, we may mention Antiphon's common practice of passing from
the copulative to the adversative. He often begins with καί, but substitutes a δέ
for the corresponding καί which should follow. This represents the two members
as at first corresponding parts of a whole, and thus the opposition of the second to
the first is rendered more prominent and striking.

‖ λέξις εἰρομένη.

are, indeed, plenty of long sentences in these authors, in which they
show a power of bringing thoughts and observations into the right connexion with each other.   But these long sentences appear as a heaping
together of thoughts without any necessary rule or limit, such that if
the author had known any further circumstances likely to support his
argument, he might have added or incorporated those circumstances,[*]
and not as a whole of which all the subordinate particulars were necessary integral parts.   The only structure of sentences which was cultivated
to any great extent at this period was that in which the different members are not related to one another as principal or subordinate but merely
as consecutive sentences, *i. e.* the copulative, adversative, and disjunctive
sentences ; [†] and these were consistently and artfully carried out in all
their parts.   It is indeed very worthy of remark, how skilfully an orator
like Antiphon arranged his thoughts so that they always produced those
binary combinations of corresponding or opposed members ; and how
laboriously he strove to exhibit on every side this symmetrical relation,
and, like an architect, carried the symmetry through all the details of
his work.   To take an example, the orator has scarcely opened his mouth
to speak on the murder of Herodes when he falls into a system of paral-
lelisms such as we have just described : " Would that my oratorical skill
and knowledge of affairs, O judges, were equal to my unhappy condition
and the misfortunes which I have suffered.   As it is, however, I have
more of the latter than I ought to have ; whereas the former fails me
more than is expedient for me.   For where I was in bodily peril on
account of an unjust accusation, there my knowledge of affairs was of no
avail ; and now that I have to save my life by a true statement of the
case, I am injured by my inability to speak ;" and so forth.   It is clear
that this symmetrical structure of sentences [‡] must have had its origin in
a very peculiar bias of mind ; namely, in the habitual proneness to compare and discriminate, to place the different points of a subject in such
connexion that their likeness or dissimilitude might appear in the most
marked manner ; in a word, this mode of writing presumes that peculiar
combination of ingenuity and shrewdness for which the old Athenians
were so pre-eminently distinguished.   At the same time it cannot be
denied that the habit of speaking in this way had something misleading
in it, and that this parallelism of the members of a sentence was often
carried much farther than the natural conditions of thought would have
prescribed ; especially as a mere formal play with sounds united itself

* This structure of sentences, which occurs principally in narrative, will be
discussed more at length when we come to Thucydides.

† The sentences with και (τε) —και, with μεν —δη, with ή (πότερον) —ή. In
general, this constitutes the ἀντικειμένη λέξις.

‡ This is the ἱπερμόνως σύνθεσις of Cæcilius of Calacte (*Photius, Cod.* 259), the
concinnitas of Cicero.

guilty, whether truly or falsely, but was obliged to leave Athens. From
this time he occupied himself with commercial transactions, which he
carried on chiefly in Cyprus, and with endeavours to get recalled from
banishment; until, on the downfal of the thirty tyrants, he returned to
his native city under the protection of the general amnesty which the
opposing parties had sworn to observe. Though he was not without
molestation on account of the old charge, we find him still engaged in
public affairs, till at last, being sent as ambassador to Sparta in the
course of the Corinthian war, in order to negotiate a peace, he was again
banished by the Athenians because the result of his negotiations was
unsatisfactory.

We have three remaining speeches by Andocides : the first relating to
his return from exile, and delivered after the restoration of the democracy
by the overthrow of the Four hundred counsellors; the second relating to
the mysteries, and delivered in Ol. 95, 1. B.C. 400, in which Andocides
endeavours to confute the continually reviving charge with respect to the
profanation of the mysteries, by going back to the origin of the whole
matter; the third on the peace with Lacedæmon, delivered in Ol. 97, 1.
B.C. 392, in which the orator urges the Athenian assembly to conclude
peace with the Spartans. The genuineness of the last speech is doubted
even by the old grammarians : but the speech against Alcibiades, the
object of which is to get Alcibiades ostracized instead of the orator, is
undoubtedly spurious. If the speech were genuine it could not have
been written by Andocides consistently with the well-known circumstances relating to the ostracism of Alcibiades : in that case it must be
assigned to Phæax, who shared with Alcibiades in the danger of ostracism; and this is the opinion of a modern critic :* but the contents and
form of the speech prove beyond all power of confutation that it is an
imitation by some later rhetorician.†

Although Andocides has been included in the list of the ten celebrated
orators, he is very inferior to the others in talent and art.‡ He exhibits
neither any particular acuteness in treating the great events which are
referred to in his speeches, nor that precision in the connexion of his
thoughts which marks all the other writers of this time : yet we must
give him credit for his freedom from the mannerism into which the more
distinguished men of the age so easily fell, and also for a sort of natural
liveliness, which may together be considered as reliques of the austere
style, as it appears in Antiphon and Thucydides. §

* Taylor (*Lectiones Lysiacæ*, c. VI.), who has not been refuted by Ruhnken and
Valckenaer.—[See Thirlwall, *Hist. of Greece*, III., p. 463.—ED.]

† According to Meier, *de Andocidis quæ vulgo fertur oratione in Alcibiadem*, a
series of programmes of the University of Halle.

‡ It is surprising that Critias was not rather enrolled among the Ten, but perhaps
his having been one of the Thirty stood in his way. Comp. Chap. XXXI. § 4.

§ The ἀντικειμένη λέξις prevails in Andocides also, but without any striving after
symmetry of expression.

CHAPTER XXXIV.

§ 1. The life of Thucydides: his training that of the age of Pericles. § 2. His new method of treating history. § 3. The consequent distribution and arrangement of his materials, as well in his whole work as, § 4, in the introduction. § 5. His mode of treating these materials; his research and criticism. § 6. Accuracy and, § 7, intellectual character of his history. §§ 8, 9. The speeches considered as the soul of his history. §§ 10, 11. His mode of expression and the structure of his sentences.

§ 1. THUCYDIDES, an Athenian of the demus of Alimus, was born in Ol. 77, 2. B.C. 471, nine years after the battle of Salamis.* His father Olorus, or Orolus, has a Thracian name, although Thucydides himself was an Athenian born: his mother Hegesipyle bears the same name as the Thracian wife of the great Miltiades, the conqueror at Marathon; and through her Thucydides was connected with the renowned family of the Philaidæ. This family from the time of the older Miltiades, who left Athens during the tyranny of the Pisistratidæ and founded a principality of his own in the Thracian Chersonese, had formed alliances with the people and princes of that district; the younger Miltiades, the Marathonian victor, had married the daughter of a Thracian king named Orolus; the children of this marriage were Cimon and the younger Hegesipyle, the latter of whom married the younger Orolus, probably a grandson of the first, who had obtained the rights of citizenship at Athens through his connexions; the son of this marriage was Thucydides. †

In this way Thucydides belonged to a distinguished and powerful family, possessed of great riches, especially in Thrace. Thucydides himself owned some gold-mines in that country, namely, at *Scapte-Hyle*

---

* According to the well known statement of Pamphila (a learned woman of Nero's time), cited by Gellius, *N. A.* XV., 23. This statement is not impugned by what Thucydides says himself (V., 26), that he was of the right age to observe the progress of the Peloponnesian war. He might well say this of the period between the 40th and 67th years of his life; for though the ἡλικία in reference to military service was different, it seems that the ancients placed the age suitable to literary labours at a more advanced point than we do.

† This is the best way of reconciling the statements of Marcellinus (*vita Thucydidis*) and Suidas with the well-known historical data. The following is the whole genealogy:—

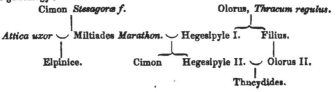

Cimon *Stesagoræ f.*   Olorus, *Thracum regulus.*

Attica uxor ⌣ Miltiades *Marathon.* ⌣ Hegesipyle I.   Filius.

Elpinice.   Cimon   Hegesipyle II. ⌣ Olorus II.

Thucydides.

quently, he had excluded everything pertaining either to the foreign
relations or the internal policy of the different states which did not bear
upon the great contest for the *Hegemony*, or chief power in Greece: but,
on the other hand, he has admitted everything, to whatever part of Hellas
it referred, which was connected with this strife of nations. From the
first, Thucydides had considered this war as a great event in the history
of the world, as one which could not be ended without deciding the
question, whether Athens was to become a great empire, or whether
she was to be reduced to the condition of an ordinary Greek republic,
surrounded by many others equally free and equally powerful: he could
not but see that the peace of Nicias, which was concluded after the first
ten years of the war, had not really put an end to it; that it was but
interrupted by an equivocal and ill-observed armistice, and that it
broke out afresh during the Sicilian expedition: with the zeal of an
interested party, and with all the power of truth, he shows that all this
was one great contest, and that the peace was not a real one.*

§ 3. Thucydides has distributed and arranged his materials according
to this conception of his subject. The war itself is divided according to
the mode in which it was carried on, and which was regulated among
the Greeks, more than with us, by the seasons of the year: the campaigns
were limited to the summer; the winter was spent in preparing the
armaments and in negotiation. As the Greeks had no general æra, and
as the calendar of each country was arranged according to some peculiar
cycle, Thucydides takes his chronological dates from the sequence of
the seasons, and from the state of the corn-lands, which had a considerable influence on the military proceedings; such expressions as,
" when the corn was in ear," or " when the corn was ripe," † were sufficient to mark the coherence of events with all needful accuracy. In his
history of the different campaigns, Thucydides endeavours to avoid
interruptions to the thread of his narrative: in describing any expedition,
whether by land or sea, he tries to keep the whole together, and prefers
to violate the order of time, either by going back or by anticipating
future events, in order to escape the confusion resulting from continually
breaking off and beginning again. That long and protracted affairs, like
the sieges of Potidæa and Platæa, must recur in different parts of the
history is unavoidable; indeed it could not be otherwise, even if the
distribution into summers and winters could have been given up. ‡ For
transactions like the siege of Potidæa cannot be brought to an end in
a luminous and satisfactory manner without a complete view of the
position of the belligerent powers, which prevented the besieged from

---

* Thucyd. V. 26.   † περὶ ἐκβολὴν σίτου, ἀκμάζοντος τοῦ σίτου, &c.
‡ This is in answer to the censures of Dionysius, *de Thucydide judicium*, c. IX.,
p. 826, Reiske.

receiving succour. The careful reader of Thucydides will never be
disturbed by any violent break in the history : and the event which,
considered as one, was the most momentous in the whole war, and
which the author has invested with the most lively interest,—namely,
the Athenian expedition to Sicily, with its happy commencement and
ruinous termination,—is told with but few (and those short) digressions.*
The whole work, if it had been completed, would resolve itself into three
nearly equal divisions : I. The war up to the peace of Nicias, which
from the forays of the Spartans under Archidamus is called the Archi-
damian war ; II. The restless movements among the Greek states after
the peace of Nicias, and the commencement of the Sicilian expedition ;
III. The renewed war with the Peloponnesus, called by the ancients the
Decelean war, down to the fall of Athens. According to the division
into books, which, though not made by Thucydides, proceeded from an
arrangement by some intelligent grammarians, the first third is made up
of books II. III. IV. ; the second of books V. VI. VII. ; of the third,
Thucydides himself has completed only one book, the VIIIth.

§ 4. In discussing the manner in which Thucydides distributed and
arranged his materials, we have still to speak of the 1st book ; indeed
this demands a more particular consideration, because its arrangement
depends less upon the subject itself than upon Thucydides' peculiar
reflections. The author begins with asserting that the Peloponnesian
war was the greatest event that had happened within the memory of
man, and establishes this by a retrospective survey of the more ancient
history of Greece, including the Persian war. He goes through the
oldest period, the traditions of the Trojan war, the centuries immediately
following that event, and, finally, the Persian invasion, and shows that
all previous undertakings wanted the external resources which were
brought into play during the Peloponnesian war, because they were
deficient in two things,—money and a navy,†—which did not arise
among the Greeks till a late period, and developed themselves only by
slow degrees. In this way Thucydides applies historically the maxims
which Pericles had practically impressed upon the Athenians, that
money and ships, not territory and population, ought to be made the
basis of their power ; and the Peloponnesian war itself appeared to
him a great proof of this position, because the Peloponnesians, notwithstanding their superiority in extent of country and in the number of their
free citizens, so long fought with Athens at a disadvantage till their
alliance with Persia had furnished them with abundant pecuniary resources, and thus enabled them to collect and maintain a considerable

* How happily even these digressions are interwoven with the narrative of the
Sicilian expedition ; *e. g.*, the calamities produced at Athens by the occupation of
Decelea, and the horrible massacre at Mycalessus by the Thracian mercenaries
(Thucyd. VII. 27—30).   † χρήματα καὶ ναυτικόν.

Xenophon: only we must not seek to raise any doubt as to the genuineness of the VIIIth book; all that we are entitled to do is to explain, on this hypothesis, certain differences in the composition, and to infer from this that the work wants the last touches of the master's hand.[*]

§ 6. We cannot form any opinion as to the manner in which Thucydides collected, compared, examined, and put together his materials, for the oral traditions of the time are lost: but, if perfect clearness in the narrative; if the consistency of every detail as well with other parts of the history as with all we know from other sources of the state of affairs at that time; if the harmony of all that he tells with the laws of nature and with the known characters of the persons of whom he writes; if all this furnishes a security for the truth and fidelity of an historian, we have this guarantee in its most ample form in the work of Thucydides. The ancients, who were very strict in estimating the characters of their own historians, and who had questioned the veracity of most of them, are unanimous in recognizing the accuracy and trustworthiness of Thucydides, and the plan of his work, considered in the spirit of a rhetorician of the time, fully justifies his principle of keeping to a statement of the truth: even the singular reproach that he has chosen too melancholy a subject, and that he has not considered the glory of his countrymen in this selection, becomes, when properly considered, an encomium on his strict historical fidelity. The deviations of later historians, especially Diodorus and Plutarch, upon close scrutiny, confirm the accuracy of Thucydides;[†] and, in all the points of contact between them, in characterizing the statesmen of the day and in describing the position of Athens at different times, Thucydides and Aristophanes have all the agreement which we could expect between the bold caricatures of the comedian and the accurate pictures of the historian. Indeed we will venture to say, that there is no period of history which stands before us with the same distinctness with which the first twenty-one years of the Peloponnesian war are presented to us in the work of Thucydides, where we are led through every circumstance in all its essential details, in its grounds and occasion, in its progress and results, with the utmost confidence in the guiding hand of the historian. The only thing similar to it in Roman history is Sallust's account of the Jugurthan war and of the Catilinarian conspiracy. The remains of Tacitus' contemporary history (the *Historiæ*), although equally complete in the details, are very inferior in clear and definite narratives of fact. Tacitus hastens from one exciting occurrence to another, without waiting to give an adequate account of

---

[*] On the speeches wanting in this book, see below, § 11.

[†] Diodorus, in the history of the period between the Persian and Peloponnesian wars, though he adopts the annalistic mode of reckoning, is far from being as exact as Thucydides, who only gives a few notes of time. All that we can use in Diodorus is his leading dates, successions of kings, years of the deaths of individuals, &c.

HISTORY OF SWITZERLAND.

The following are the Contents of this Work; and it is illustrated by a Map, coloured so as to show the gradual Increase of the Swiss Confederation:—

Price, in cloth boards, 7s. 6d.

WORKS OF THE SOCIETY.

THE STARS ON THE GNOMONIC PROJECTION.

In Six large Maps, measuring 29 inches by 27 inches. Edited by
Sir J. W. Lubbock.
Price 1l. 1s. Coloured, and 15s. Plain.

In the Press,

A GENERAL REPORT of MECHANICS' INSTITUTIONS in ENGLAND.

It will contain a List of such Institutions, and of Lecturers, &c.

HISTORY OF ROME.

The Fifth Number of the History of Rome under the Emperors
will be published in September.

Second Period, b.c. 390 to b.c. 31, by W. B. Donne, Esq. The
First Number of this Division of the Work will be published on the 1st
of August.

THE THEORY OF EQUATIONS.

By the Rev. Robert Murphy, A.M.
Price 4s.

. London: Printed by William Clowes and Sons, Stamford Street.

LIBRARY OF USEFUL KNOWLEDGE.

HISTORY OF THE
LITERATURE OF GREECE.
VOL. II.—PART IV.

COMMITTEE.

Chairman—The Right Hon. LORD BROUGHAM, F.R.S., Member of the
National Institute of France.
Vice-Chairman—The Right Hon. EARL SPENCER.
Treasurer—JOHN WOOD, Esq.

WILLIAM ALLEN, Esq., F.R. and R.A.S.
CAPTAIN BEAUFORT, R.N., F.R. and R.A.S.
GEORGE BURROWS, M.D.
PETER STAFFORD CAREY, Esq., A.M.
JOHN CONOLLY, M.D.
WILLIAM COULSON, Esq.
THE RIGHT REV. THE BISHOP OF ST. DAVID's, D.D.
J. F. DAVIS, Esq., F.R.S.
Sir H. T. DE LA BECHE, F.R.S.
THE RIGHT HON. LORD DENMAN.
SAMUEL DUCKWORTH, Esq.
THE RIGHT REV. THE BISHOP OF DURHAM, D.D.
T. F. ELLIS, Esq., A.M., F.R.A.S.
JOHN ELLIOTSON, M.D., F.R.S.
THE RIGHT HON. GEORGE EVANS.
THOMAS FALCONER, Esq.
JOHN FORBES, M.D., F.R.S.
Sir I. L. GOLDSMID, Bart., F.R. and R.A.S.
FRANCIS HENRY GOLDSMID, Esq.
B. GOMPERTZ, Esq., F.R. and R.A.S.
J. T. GRAVES, Esq., A.M., F.R.S.
G. B. GREENOUGH, Esq., F.R. and L.S.
SIR EDMUND HEAD, Bart., A.M.
M. D. HILL, Esq., Q.C.
ROWLAND HILL, Esq., F.R.A.S.
RIGHT HON. SIR J. C. HOBHOUSE, Bart., M.P.
THOMAS HODGKIN, M.D.

DAVID JARDINE, Esq., A.M.
HENRY B. KER, Esq.
THOMAS HEWITT KEY, Esq., A.M.
SIR CHARLES LEMON, Bart., M.P.
GEORGE C. LEWIS, Esq., A.M.
JAMES LOCH, Esq., M.P., F.G.S.
GEORGE LONG, Esq., A.M.
HENRY MALDEN, Esq., A.M.
ARTHUR T. MALKIN, Esq., A.M.
MR. SERJEANT MANNING.
R. I. MURCHISON, Esq., F.R.S., F.G.S.
THE RIGHT HON. LORD NUGENT.
W. SMITH O'BRIEN, Esq., M.P.
RICHARD QUAIN, Esq.
P. M. ROGET, M.D., Sec. R.S., F.R.A.S.
R. W. ROTHMAN, Esq., A.M.
SIR MARTIN A. SHEE, P.R.A., F.R.S.
SIR GEORGE T. STAUNTON, Bart.
JOHN TAYLOR, Esq., F.R.S.
A. T. THOMSON, M.D.
THOMAS VARDON, Esq.
JACOB WALEY, Esq., B.A.
JAMES WALKER, Esq., F.R.S.
HENRY WAYMOUTH, Esq.
THOMAS WEBSTER, Esq., A.M.
RIGHT HON. LORD WROTTESLEY, A.M., F.R.A.S
JOHN ASHTON YATES, Esq.

THOMAS COATES, Esq., *Secretary*, 59, Lincoln's Inn Fields.

LONDON:
PUBLISHED BY CHAPMAN & HALL, 186, STRAND.

No. 351.]   *August* 1, 1842.   [*Price Sixpence.*

UNDER THE SUPERINTENDENCE OF THE SOCIETY FOR THE
DIFFUSION OF USEFUL KNOWLEDGE.

Published every alternate month, price 7s. 6d. each Number,

A Series of

DIAGRAMS,

ILLUSTRATIVE OF

THE PRINCIPLES OF MECHANICAL AND NATURAL PHILOSOPHY
AND THEIR PRACTICAL APPLICATION:

**DRAWN ON STONE BY HENRY CHAPMAN.
PRINTED IN COLOURS BY C. F. CHEFFINS.**

*Each Number will contain Three Plates (26½ inches by 19) and the series will
commence with* MECHANICS, *which will be comprised in Seven Numbers.*

No. I.—THE LEVER.
No. II.—WHEEL AND AXLE.

THE practical application of the principles of Mechanical and Natural
Philosophy is a branch of education towards which little assistance of
the kind now proposed has hitherto been rendered. The ordinary sources
of information on these subjects are either books in which principles
are enunciated, illustrated by diagrams rather of a theoretical than of
a practical character, and of too small dimensions to be used for the instruction of several persons at the same time, or lectures orally delivered,
and illustrated by actual experiment, requiring expensive apparatus and
arrangements not within the means of families and schools. It has
appeared to the COMMITTEE that Drawings or Diagrams, of a sufficient size
to be used for the purposes of Class instruction, might be made to contribute very much to these objects. With this view it is intended to furnish
large and accurate representations of the more simple instruments and
machines and their combinations in actual use. Descriptions (to be published separately) will be given of the construction of the machines and of
the principles upon which they depend, and which the Diagrams are
designed to illustrate. Such descriptions will enable any person possessing
only a limited knowledge of the subject to convey correct information to
those whom he may have to instruct, and will serve as a comprehensive
syllabus or outline of lectures for the more extended object of Class
instruction.

This Series will also, it is conceived, be extremely useful to classes in
which Civil Engineering is taught, and to those who are seeking for instruction in mechanical drawing, as the Diagrams are drawn to a scale, and with
sufficient accuracy of detail to serve as working drawings.

the more common events connected with them.* Thucydides himself designed his work for those who wish to learn the truth of what
has happened, and to know what is most for their interest in reference
to the similar cases, which, according to the course of human affairs,
must again occur ; for such persons Thucydides bequeaths his book
as a lasting study.† In this there is an early indication of the
tendency to *pragmatical history*, in which the chief object was the training of generals and statesmen,—in a word, the *practical* application of
the work ; while the narration of events was regarded as merely a means
to an end : such a pragmatical history we shall find in the later ages of
ancient literature.

§ 7. Thucydides would never have been able to attain this truth and
clearness in his history had he contented himself with merely setting
down the simple testimonies of eye-witnesses, who described what they
saw and felt, and had only inserted here and there his own views and
reasonings. Its credibility rests mainly on the circumstance, that
Thucydides, as well by education as by his natural abilities, was
capable of inferring, from the conduct of the persons who figure in his
history, the motives which actuated them on every occasion. It is only
in particular cases, where he expressly mentions his doubts, that Thucydides leaves us in the dark with regard to the motives of the persons
whose actions he describes ; and he gives us these motives, not as matter
of supposition and conjecture, but as matter of fact. As an honest
and conscientious man, he could not have done this unless he had
been convinced that these views and considerations. and these alone,
had guided the persons in question. Thucydides very seldom delivers
his own opinion, as such ; still more rarely does he pronounce sentence
on the morality or immorality of a given action. Every person who
appears in this history has a strongly marked character, and the more
significant his share in the main action, so much the more clearly is he
stamped with the mark of individuality ; and though we cannot but
admire the skill and power with which Thucydides is able to sum up in
a few words the characters of certain individuals, such as Themistocles,
Pericles, Brasidas, Nicias, Alcibiades, yet we must admire still more the
nicety with which he has kept up and carried out all the characters, in
every feature of their actions, and of the thoughts and opinions which
guided them.‡

* For instance, it is extremely difficult to get an entirely clear conception of the
war in Upper-Italy, between the partisans of Otho and Vitellius.
† This is the meaning of the celebrated κτῆμα ἰς ἀεί, I. 22 : it does not mean an
everlasting memorial or monument. Thucydides opposes his work, which people
were to keep by them and read over and over again, to a composition which was
designed to gratify an audience on one occasion only.
‡ Marcellinus calls Thucydides δεινὸς ἠθογραφῆσαι, as Sophocles, among the poets,
was also renowned for the ἠθοποιῖν.

§ 8. The most decided and the boldest proof which Thucydides has
given of his intention to set forth the events of the war in all their secret
workings, is manifested in that part of his history which is most peculiarly his own—the *speeches*. It is true that these speeches, given in
the words of the speakers, are much more natural to an ancient historian
than they would be to one at the present day. Speeches delivered in the
public assembly, in federal meetings, or before the army, were often, by
virtue of the consequences springing from them, important events, and
at the same time so public, that nothing but the infirmities of human
memory could prevent them from being preserved and communicated
to others. Hence it came to pass, that the Greeks, who in the greater
liveliness of their disposition were accustomed to look to the form as well
as to the substance of every public communication, in relating the circumstance were not content with giving an abstract of the subject of the
speech, or the opinions of the speaker in their own words, but introduced
the orator himself as speaking. As in such a case, the narrator supplied
a good deal from his own head, when his memory could not make good
the deficiency; so Thucydides does not give us an exact report of the
speeches which he introduces, because he could not have recollected perfectly even those which he heard himself. He explains his own intention in this matter, by telling us that he endeavoured to keep as closely
as possible to the true report of what was actually said; but, when this
was unattainable, he had made the parties speak what was most to the
purpose in reference to the matter in hand.* We must, however, go a
step further than Thucydides, and concede to him greater freedom from
literal tradition than he was perhaps conscious of himself. The speeches
in Thucydides contain a sum of the motives and causes which led to
the principal transactions; namely, the opinions of individuals and of the
different parties in a state, from which these transactions sprung.
Speeches are introduced whenever he thinks it necessary to introduce
such a developement of causes: when there is no such necessity, the
speeches are omitted; though perhaps just as many were actually delivered in the one case as in the other. Accordingly the speeches
which he has given contain, in a summary form, much that was
really spoken on various occasions; as, for instance, in the *second*
debate in the Athenian assembly about the mode of treating the conquered Mitylenæans, in which the decree that was really acted on was
passed by the people; in this the opinions of the opposing parties—the
violently tyrannical, and the milder and more humane party—are pour-
trayed in the speeches of Cleon and Diodotus, though Cleon had, the
day before, carried the first inhuman decree against the Mitylenæans,†
and in so doing had doubtless said much in support of his motion which

---

* τὰ δέοντα μάλιστα, Thucyd. I. 22.   † Thucyd. IIL. 36.

Thucydides has probably introduced into his speech in the second day's debate.* In one passage, Thucydides gives us a dialogue instead of a speech, because the circumstances scarcely admitted of any public harangue :. this occurs in the negotiations between the Athenians and the council of Melos, before the Athenian attack upon this Dorian island, after the peace of Nicias : but Thucydides takes this opportunity of stating the point at which the Athenians had arrived in the grasping, selfish, and tyrannical policy, which guided their dealings with the minor states.†

§ 9. It is unnecessary to mention that we must not look for any mimic representation in the speeches of Thucydides, any attempt to depict the mode of speaking peculiar to different nations and individuals ; if he had done this, his whole work would have lost its unity of tone and its harmony of colouring. Thucydides goes into the characteristics of · the persons whom he introduces as speaking, only so far as the general law of his history permits. In setting forth the views of his speakers, he has regard to their character, not only in the contents and subject of the speeches which he assigns to them, but also in the mode in which he developes and connects their thoughts. To take the first book alone, we have admirable pictures of the Corcyræans, who only maintain the mutual *advantages* resulting from their alliance with Athens ; of the Corinthians, who rely in some degree on moral grounds ; of the discretion, mature wisdom, and noble simplicity of the excellent Archidamus ; and of the haughty self-confidence of the Ephor Sthenelaidas, a Spartan of the lower order : the tone of the composition agrees entirely with the views and fundamental ideas of their speeches ; as, for instance, the searching copiousness of Archidamus and the cutting brevity of Sthenelaidas. The chief concern of Thucydides in the composition of these speeches was to exhibit the principles which guided the conduct of the persons of whom he is writing, and to allow their opinions to exhibit, confirm, and justify or exculpate themselves. This is done with such intrinsic truth and consistency, the historian identifies himself so entirely with the characters which he describes, and gives such support and plausibility to their views and sentiments, that we may be sure that the

* The speeches often stand in a relation to one another which could not have been justified by existing circumstances. Thus, the speech of the Corinthians in I. 120 seqq., is a direct answer to the speech of Archidamus in the Spartan assembly, and to that of Pericles at Athens, although the Corinthians did not hear either of them. The reason of this relation is, that the speech of the Corinthians expresses the hopes of victory entertained by one portion of the Peloponnesians, while Archidamus and Pericles view the unfavourable position of the Peloponnese with equal clearness, but from different points of view. Compare also the remarks on the speeches of Pericles in Chap. XXXI.

† Dionysius says (*de Thucyd. judic.*, p. 910), that the principles unfolded in this dialogue are suited to barbarians and not to Athenians, and blames Thucydides most violently for introducing them : but these were really the principles on which the Athenians acted.

persons themselves could not have pleaded their own cause better under
the immediate influence of their interests and passions.   It must indeed
be allowed, that this wonderful quality of the historian is partly due to
the sophistical exercises, which taught the art of speaking for both
parties, for the bad as well as the good; but the application which
Thucydides made of this art was the best and most beneficial that could
be conceived; and it is obvious, that there can be no true history unless
we presume such a faculty of assuming the characters of the persons
described, and giving some kind of justification to the most opposite
opinions, for without this the force of opinions can never be adequately
represented.   Thucydides developes the principles which guided the
Athenians in their dealings with their allies with such a consistent
train of reasoning, that we are almost compelled to assent to the truth
of the argument.   In a series of speeches, occurring in very different
parts of the history, but so connected with one another that we cannot
fail to recognize in them a continuation of the same reasoning and a
progressive confirmation of those principles, the Athenians show that
they did not gain their power by violence, but were compelled by the
force of circumstances to give it the form of a protectorate; that in the
existing state of things they could not relinquish this protectorate without
hazarding their own existence; that as this protectorate had become a
tyranny, it must be maintained by vigour and severity; that humanity
and equity could only be appealed to in dealings with an equal, who had
an opportunity of requiting benefits conferred upon him;* till at last, in
the dialogue with the Melians, the Athenians assert the right of the
stronger as a law of nature, and rest their demand, that the Melians
should become subject to them, on this principle alone.   "We desire
and do," say they, "only what is consistent with all that men conceive
of the gods and desire for themselves.   For as we believe it of the gods,
so we clearly perceive in the case of men, that all who have the power
are constrained by a necessity of nature to govern and command.   We
did not invent this law, nor were we the first to avail ourselves of it;
but since we have received it as a law already established and in full
force, and since we shall leave it as a perpetual inheritance to those who
come after us, we intend, on the present occasion, to act in accordance
with it, because we know that you and all others would act in the same
manner if you possessed the same power."†   These principles, according
to which no doubt Greeks and other men had acted before them, though
perhaps under some cloak or disguise of justice, are so coolly propounded

* Thucyd. III. 37. 40.   This is said by Cleon, who, in the case in question,
was defeated by the more humane party of Diodotus; but this exception, made in
the case of the Mitylenæans, remained an exception in favour of humanity; as a
general rule, the spirit of Cleon predominated in the foreign policy of Athens.
   † Thucyd. V. 105, according to Dr. Arnold's correct interpretation.

by the historian in this dialogue, he has delivered them so calmly and dispassionately, so absolutely without any expression of his own opinion to the contrary, that we are almost led to believe that Thucydides recognized the right of the strongest as the only rule of politics. But there is clearly a wide difference between the modes of thinking and acting which Thucydides describes with such indifference as prevalent in Athens, and his own convictions as to what was for the advantage of mankind in general and of his own countrymen in particular. How little Thucydides, as an honest man, approved of the maxims of Athenian policy established in his own time, is clear from his striking and instructive picture of the changes which took place in the political conduct of the different states after the first years of the war, in consequence chiefly of the domestic strife of factions—changes which Thucydides never intended to represent as beneficial, for he says of them, that "simplicity of character, which is the principal ingredient in a noble nature, was in those days ridiculed and banished from the world." * The panegyric on the Athenian democracy and on their mode of living, which occurs chiefly in the funeral oration of Pericles, is modified considerably by the assertion of Thucydides, that the government of the Five-thousand was the best administered constitution which the Athenians had enjoyed in his time ;† and also by the incidental remark that the Lacedæmonians and Chians alone, so far as he knew, were the only people who had been able to unite moderation and discretion with their good fortune.‡ And thus, in general, we must draw a distinction between the sound and serious morality of Thucydides and the impartial love of truth, which led him to paint the world as it was ; and we must not deny him a deep religious feeling, because his plan was to describe human affairs according to their relation of cause and effect ; and because, while he took account of the belief of others as a motive of their actions, he does not obtrude his own belief on the subject. Religion, mythology, and poetry, are subjects which Thucydides, with a somewhat partial view of the matter, § sets aside as foreign to the business of a historian ; and we may justly regard him as the Anaxagoras of history, for he has detached the workings of Providence from the chain of causes which influence the life of man as distinctly and decidedly as the Ionian philosopher separated the νοῦς from the powers which operate on the material world. ∥

§ 10. The style and peculiar diction of Thucydides are so closely

---

* III. 83 : τὸ εὔηθες, οὗ τὸ γενναῖον πλεῖστον μετέχει, καταγελασθὲν ἠφανίσθη.
† Thucyd. VIII. 97.   ‡ Thucyd. VIII. 24.
§ It would be easy to show that Thucydides sets too low a value on the old civilization of Greece; and, in general, the first part of the first book, the introduction properly so called, as it is written to establish a general proposition for which Thucydides pleads as an advocate, does not exhibit those unprejudiced views for which the main part of the work is so peculiarly distinguished.
∥ See Vol. I., p. 247.

connected with the character of his history, and are so remarkable in themselves, that we cannot but make an attempt, notwithstanding the necessary brevity of this sketch, to set them before the reader in their main features.

We think we have already approximated to a right conception of this peculiar style, in the remark, that in Thucydides the concise and pregnant oratory of Pericles was combined with the antique and vigorous but artificial style of Antiphon's rhetoric.

In the use of words, Thucydides is distinct and precise, and every word which he uses is significant and expressive. Even in him this degenerates, in some passages, into an attempt to make distinctions, after the manner of Prodicus, in the use of nearly synonymous words. *

This definiteness of expression is aided by great copiousness of diction, and in this, Thucydides, like Antiphon, uses a great number of antique, poetical words, not for the mere purpose of ornament, as is the case with Gorgias, but because the language of the day sanctioned the use of these pithy and expressive phrases.† In his dialect, Thucydides kept closer to the old Attic forms than his contemporaries among the comic poets.‡

Similarly, the constructions in Thucydides are marked by a freedom, which, on the whole, is more suitable to antique poetry than to prose; and this has enabled him to form connexions of ideas, without an admixture of superfluous words, which disturb the connexion, and, consequently, with greater distinctness than would be possible with more limited and regular constructions. An instance of this is the liberty of construing verbal-nouns in the same way as the verbs from which they are derived.§ These, and other things of the same kind, produce that *rapidity of description*, as the ancients call it,‖ which hits the mark at once.

In the order of the words, too, Thucydides takes a liberty which is generally conceded to poets alone; inasmuch as he sometimes arranges the ideas rather according to their real connexion or contrast than according to the grammatical construction. ¶

---

* I. 69; II. 62; III. 16. 39.

† These expressions, which had become obsolete in the mean time, were called in later times γλῶσσαι; hence, Dionysius complains of the γλωσσηματικὸν in the style of Thucydides.

‡ See Chap. XXVII. at the end.

§ This is the origin of such expressions as the following: ἢ οὐ περιτείχισις, "the circumstance that a hostile city was not surrounded by walls of circumvallation;" τὸ αὐτὸ ὑπὸ ἁπάντων ἰδίᾳ δόξασμα, "the case in which every individual, each for himself, entertains the same opinion;" ἡ ἀκινδύνως δουλεία (not the same as ἀκίνδυνος), "a state of slavery in which one can live comfortably and free from all apprehensions."

‖ τάχος τῆς σημασίας.

¶ As in III. 39: μετὰ τῶν πολεμιωτάτων ἡμᾶς στάντις διαφθεῖραι, where the first words are placed together for the sake of contrast.

In the connection of his sentences there is sometimes an inequality and harshness,* very different from the smooth and polished style of later times. Moreover he does not avoid using different grammatical forms (cases and moods) in the corresponding members of the sentence, † or allowing rapid changes in the grammatical structure, which are often not expressly indicated but tacitly introduced, an expression required by the sentence being supplied from another similar one. ‡

§ 11. The structure of periods in Thucydides, like that of Antiphon, stands half-way between the loose connexion of sentences in the Ionian writers and the periodic style which subsequently developed itself at Athens. The greater power and energy in the combination of thoughts is manifested by the greater length of the sentences. In Thucydides there are two species of periods, which are both of them equally characteristic of his style. In one of them, which may be termed *the descending period*, the action, or result, is placed first, and is immediately followed by the causes or motives expressed by causal-sentences, or participles, which are again confirmed by similar forms of speech. § The other form, *the ascending period*, begins with the primary circumstances, developing from them all sorts of consequences, or reflexions referring to them, and concludes, often after a long chain of consequences, with the result, the determination, or the action itself. ‖ Both descriptions of periods produce a feeling of difficulty, and require to be read twice in order to be understood clearly and in all respects ; it is possible to make them more immediately intelligible, more convenient and pleasant to read, by breaking them up into the smaller clauses suggested by the pauses in the sentence ; but then we shall be forced to confess that when the difficulty is once overcome, the form chosen by Thucydides conveys the strongest impression of a unity of thought and a combined working of every part to produce one result.

This mode of constructing the sentence is peculiar to the historical style of Thucydides : but he resembles the other writers of the age in

---

* ἀνωμαλία, τραχυτῆ.

† e. g., when he connects by καὶ two different constructions of cases, as the grounds of an action, or when, after the same final or conditional particle, he places first the conjunctive, and then the optative, in which the distinction is obvious.— [See Arnold's *Thucydides*, III. 22.—ED.]

‡ The σχῆμα πρὸς τὸ σημαινόμενον, also the ἀπὸ κοινοῦ, is very common in Thucydides.

§ Examples, I. 1 : Θουκυδίδης ξυνέγραψν κ.τ.λ. I. 25 : Κερίνθιοι δὲ κατὰ τὸ δίκαιον ἤρχοντο πολεμεῖν and everywhere.

‖ Examples, I. 2 : τῆς γὰρ ἐμπορίας κ.τ.λ. I. 58 : Ποτιδαιᾶται δὲ πέμψαντες κ.τ.λ. IV. 73, 74 : οἱ γὰρ Μεγαρῆς—ἔρχονται. It is interesting to observe how Dionysius (de *Thucyd. judic.*, p. 872) subjects these ascending periods to his criticism, and resolves them into more intelligible and pleasing, but less vigorous forms, by taking out of the middle a number of the subordinate clauses and adding them, by way of appendix, at the end. Antiphon resembles Thucydides in this particular also ; e. g. in the sentence (*Tetral.* I. α. § 6) : ἐκ παλαιοῦ γὰρ κ.τ.λ.

the symmetrical structure which prevails in his speeches, in separating
and contrasting the different ideas, in comparing and discriminating, in
looking backwards and forwards at the same time, and so producing a
sort of equilibrium both in the diction and in the thoughts. As we have
already said, in speaking of Antiphon, this antithetical style is not mere
mannerism; it is a natural product of the acuteness of the people
of Attica; but at the same time it is not to be denied, that under
the influence of the sophistical rhetoric it degenerated into a sort of
mannerism; and Thucydides himself is full of artifices of such a nature
that we are sometimes at a loss whether we are to admire his refined discrimination, or wonder at his antique and affected ornaments,—especially
when the outward graces of *Isocola, Homœoteleuta, Parecheses,* &c., are
superadded to the real contrasts of thoughts and ideas.*

On the other hand, Thucydides, even more than Antiphon, is free
from all those irregularities of diction which proceed from passion or
dissimulation; he is conspicuous for a sort of equable tranquillity, which
cannot be better described than by comparing it to that sublime serenity
of soul which marks the features of all the gods and heroes sculptured
by Phidias and his school. It is not an imperfection of language, it is
rather a mark of dignity, which predominates in every expression, and
which, even in the most perilous straits which necessarily called into play
every passion and emotion—fear and anguish, indignation and hatred—
even in these cases, bids the speaker maintain a tone of moderation and reflexion, and, above all, constrains him to content himself with a plain and
impressive statement of the affair which he has in hand. What passionate
declamation a later rhetorician would have put into the mouths of the
Theban and Platæan orators, when the latter are pleading for life and
death against the former before the Spartans, and yet Thucydides introduces only one burst of emotion: " Have you not done a dreadful
deed?" †

It will readily be imagined, on the slightest comparison between these
speeches and those of Lysias, how strange this style and this eloquence
—with its fulness of thoughts, its terse and nervous diction, and its connexions of sentences not to be understood without the closest attention—
must have appeared to the Athenians, even at the time when the work

---

* As when Thucydides says (IV. 61): ἃ τ' ἐπίκλητοι εὐπρεπῶς ἄδικοι
ἐλθόντες, εὐλόγως ἄπρακτοι ἀπίασιν ι. ι., "and thus those who with specious
pretexts came here on an unjust invitation, will be sent away on good grounds
without having effected their object." We have other examples in I. 77. 144;
III. 38. 57. 82; IV. 108. The old rhetoricians often speak of these σχήματα τῆς
λέξεως in Thucydides; Dionysius thinks them μειρακιώδη, *puerilia.* Compare Aulus
Gellius, *N. A.,* XVIII. 8.

† Πῶς οἱ δεινὰ εἰργασθε; III. 66. There is a good deal more liveliness and cheerfulness (probably intended to characterize the speaker) in the oration of Athena-
goras, the leader of the democratic party at Syracuse. (Thucyd. VI. 38, 39.)

of Thucydides first began to attract notice. In reference to the speeches, Cratippus—a continuer of the history—was perhaps right when he assigned, as a reason for the omission of speeches in the VIIIth book, that Thucydides found them no longer suited to the prevailing taste.* Even at that time these speeches must· have produced much the same effect upon the Attic taste as that which Cicero, at a later period, endeavoured to convey to the Romans, by comparing the style of Thucydides with old, sour, and heavy Falernian.† Thucydides was scarcely easier to the later Greeks and Romans than he is to the Greek scholars of the present time ; nay, when Cicero declares that he finds the speeches in his history almost unintelligible, modern philologers may well congratulate themselves that they have surmounted all these difficulties, and left scarcely anything in them unexplained or misunderstood.

CHAPTER XXXV.

§ 1. Events which followed the Peloponnesian war. The adventures of Lysias. Leading epochs of his life. § 2. The earlier sophistical rhetoric of Lysias. § 3. The style of this rhetoric preserved in his later panegyrical speeches. § 4. Change in the oratory of Lysias produced by his own impulses and by his employment as a writer of speeches for private individuals. § 5. Analysis of his speech against Agoratus. § 6. General view of his extant orations.

§ 1. THE Peloponnesian war, terminating, as it did, after enormous and unexampled military efforts, in the downfall of the power of Athens, was succeeded by a period of exhaustion and repose. Freedom and democracy were indeed restored by Thrasybulus and his party, but Athens had ceased to·be the capital of a great empire, the sovereign of the sea and of the coasts ; and it was only by the prudence of Conon that she recovered even a part of her former supremacy. The fine arts which, in the time of Pericles, had been carried to such perfection by Phidias and his school, were checked in their further progress ; and did not resume their former vigour till a generation later (Ol. 102. B.C. 372), when they sprung up into new life in the later Attic school of Praxiteles. Poetry, in the later tragedy and in the dithyramb, degenerated more and

---

* Cratippus, *apud Dionys. de Thucyd. judic.*, c. XVI., p. 847 : τοῖς ἀκούουσιν ὀχληρὰ εἶναι.
† Cicero, *Brutus* 83, § 288.

more into rhetorical casuistry or empty bombast. That higher energy, which results from a consciousness of real greatness, seemed to have vanished from the arts, as it did from the active life of man.

And yet it was at this very time that prose literature, freed from the fetters which had bound it hitherto, began a new career, which led to its fairest developement. Lysias and Isocrates (the two young men whom Socrates opposes one to another in Plato's *Phædrus*, bitterly reproaching the former, and forming the most brilliant expectations with regard to the latter) gave an entirely new form to oratory by the happy alterations which they, in different ways, introduced into the old prose style.

Lysias was descended from a family of distinction at Syracuse. His father, Cephalus, was persuaded by Pericles to settle at Athens, where he lived 30 years :* he is introduced in Plato's *Republic*, about the year Ol. 92, 2. B.C. 411,† as a very old man, respected and loved by all about him. When the great colony of Thurii was founded by an union of nearly all Greece (Ol. 84, 1. B.C. 444), Lysias went thither, along with his eldest brother Polemarchus, in order to take possession of the lot assigned to his family ; at that time he was only 15 years old. At Thurii he devoted himself to rhetoric, as taught in the school of the Sicilian Sophists ; his instructors were the well-known Tisias, and another Syracusan, named Nicias. He did not return to Athens till Ol. 92, 1. B C. 412, and lived there some few years in the house of his father Cephalus, till he set up for himself as a professed Sophist. ‡ Although he did not enjoy the rights of citizenship at Athens, but was merely a resident alien, § he and his whole family were warmly engaged in favour of the democracy. On this account, the Thirty compelled his brother Polemarchus to drink the cup of hemlock, and Lysias only escaped the rage of the tyrants by flying to Megara. He was thus all the more ready to aid Thrasybulus and the other champions of freedom at Phyle with the remains of his property, and forwarded with all his might the restoration of democracy at Athens. ||

He was now once more settled at Athens as proprietor of a shield-manufactory, also teaching rhetoric after the manner of the Sophists,

* See Lysias, *in Eratosth.*, § 4.
† According to the date of the *Republic*, as fixed by Böckh in two Programmes of the University of Berlin for the years 1838 and 1839.
‡ Λυσίας ὁ σοφιστὴς is mentioned in the speech against Neæra (p. 1352 Reiske), and there is no doubt that the orator is meant.
§ Μέτοικος. Thrasybulus wished to have made him a citizen, but circumstances did not favour his design, and the orator remained an ἰσοτελής, one of a privileged class among the μέτοικοι. As ἰσοτελεῖς the family had, before the time of the Thirty, served as choregi, like the citizens.
|| With an obvious manifestation of personal interest, Lysias (in his funeral oration, § 66) commemorates the strangers, *i. e.* the resident aliens, who fell fighting in the Peiræus by the side of the liberators of Athens.

when a new career was opened to him by an event which touched him very nearly. Eratosthenes, one of the Thirty, wished to avail himself of the advantage granted to the Thirty Tyrants under the general amnesty, namely, that it should extend to them also, if they would submit to a public inquiry, and so clear themselves of all guilt. Eratosthenes relied on having belonged to the more moderate party of Theramenes, who, on account of his greater leniency, had fallen a victim to the more energetic and violent Critias. And yet it was this very Eratosthenes who had, in accordance with a decree of the Thirty, arrested Polemarchus in the open street, carried him off to prison, and accomplished his judicial murder. When his conduct was submitted to public investigation,* Lysias came forward in person as his accuser, although, as he says himself, he had never before been in court, either on his own business or on that of any other person.† He attacks Eratosthenes, in the first instance, on account of his participation in the death of Polemarchus and the other misfortunes which he had brought upon his family; and then enters on the whole career and public life of Eratosthenes, who had also belonged to the Four-hundred, and was one of the Five Ephori whom the *Hetæriæ*, or secret associations, got elected after the battle of Ægospotami: and in this he maintains, that Theramenes, whose leniency and moderation had been so much extolled, had, by his intrigues, been a principal cause of all the calamities that had befallen the state. The whole speech is pervaded by a feeling of the strongest conviction, and by that natural warmth which we should expect in the case of a subject so immediately affecting the speaker. He concludes with a most vehement appeal to the judges: " I shall desist from any further accusations; ye have heard, seen, and experienced:—ye know!—decide then!"

§ 2. This speech forms a great epoch in the life of Lysias, in his employments and studies, in the style of his oratory, and, we may add, in the whole history of Attic prose. Up to that time, Lysias had practised rhetoric merely as a Sophist of the Sicilian school, instructing the young and composing school-exercises. The peculiarity and mannerism, which must have naturally resulted from such an application of eloquence, were the less likely to be escaped in the case of Lysias, as he was entirely under the influence of the school which had produced Gorgias. Lysias shared with Gorgias in the endeavour to evince the power of oratory, by giving probability to the improbable, and credibility to the incredible; hence resulted a love of paradox, and an unnatural and forced arrangement of the materials, excessive artifice of ornament in the details, and a total want of that natural earnestness which springs from conviction and a feeling of truth. The difference between these

---

* εὔθυνα.   † οὔτ' ἐμαυτοῦ πώποτε οὔτε ἀλλότρια πράγματα πράξας, Eratosth. § 3.

teachers of rhetoric consisted in this one feature: that Gorgias, who
had naturally a taste for smart and glittering ornaments, went much
farther than Lysias in the attempt to charm the ear with euphonies,
to captivate the imagination with splendid diction, and to blind the
understanding with the magic of oratory: whereas Lysias (who was, at
the bottom, a man of good, plain common sense, and who had imbibed
the shrewdness and refinement of an Attic mind by his constant intercourse
with the Athenians, having belonged to their party even at Thurii,*)
combined, with the usual arts of sophistic oratory, more of his own
peculiarities—more of subtle novelty in the conception, and more of
terseness and vigour in the expression.

We derive this notion of the earlier style of Lysias principally from
Plato's *Phædrus*, one of the earliest works of that great philosopher,†
the object of which is to exalt the genuine love of truth high above that
sporting with thoughts and words to which the Sophists confined themselves. The dialogue introduces us to Phædrus, a young friend of
Socrates, whom an essay of Lysias has filled with enthusiastic admiration.
This essay he reads to Socrates at his request, and partly by serious
argument, partly by a more sportive vein of reasoning, is led to recognize
the nothingness of this sort of oratory.   It is probable that Plato
did not borrow the essay in question immediately from Lysias, but
composed it himself, in order to give a comprehensive specimen of the
faults which he wished to point out.   Its theme is, to persuade a beautiful youth that he should bestow his affections upon one who loved him
not, rather than upon a lover.   As the subject of the essay is quite of a
sophistic nature, so the essay itself is merely the product of an inventive
genius, totally devoid of spirit and earnestness.   The arguments are
brought forward one after the other with the greatest exactness, but there
is no unity of thought, no general comprehension of ideas, no necessary
connexion of one part with the other; nor are the different members
grouped and massed together so as to form one consistent whole: hence,
the wearisome monotony of conjunctions by which the sentences are
linked together.‡   The prevalent collocation is the antithesis tricked out
with all its old-fashioned ornaments, the *Isocola, Homœoteleuta*, &c. §
The diction is free from the poetic ostentation of Gorgias; but it is so

---

* Lysias left Thurii when, after the failure of the Sicilian expedition, the Lace-
dæmonian party there got the upper hand, and domineered over the Athenian
colonists.

† According to the old tradition, it was written before the death of Socrates
(Ol. 95, 1. B.C. 399).

‡ In this short essay, three sentences begin with ἔτι δὲ..., and four with καὶ
μὲν δὴ...

§ In the passages (p. 233): ἐπεῖτοι γὰρ καὶ (a) ἀγαπήσουσι, καὶ (b) ἀπελευθήσουσι,
καὶ (c) τὰς θύρας ἥξουσι, καὶ (a) μάλιστα ἡσθήσονται, καὶ (β) οὐκ ἐλαχίστην χάριν εἴσονται,
καὶ (γ) πολλὰ ἀγαθὰ αὑτοῖς εὔξονται, the sentences α, β, γ are manifestly divided
into three only for the sake of an equipoise of *homœoteleuta*.

carefully formed, and with so many artificial turns, that we are at once struck with the labour which such a school-exercise must have cost the writer.

§ 3. In the extant collection of the works of Lysias we have no school-exercise (μελέτη) of this kind, and, generally, no speech anterior in date to the accusation of Eratosthenes : we have only those works which he composed in his riper years, and which exhibit the more matured taste of their author.* Among these, however, there is one which presents traces of his earlier declamation ; the reason of which is to be sought in the difference of subject. The *Funeral Oration* for the Athenians who fell in the Corinthian war, which was written by Lysias after Ol. 96, 3. B.C. 394, but could hardly have been delivered in public, belongs to a class of speeches formally distinguished from the delibera-tive† and judicial ‡ orations, because it was not designed to produce any practical result. On this very account, the sort of speeches to which we refer, and which are called " speeches for display," " show-speeches," § were removed from the influence of the impulses which imparted a freer and more natural movement to orations of the prac-tical kind. They were particularly cultivated by the Sophists, who professed to be able to praise and blame everything ; and, even after the time of the Thirty, they retained their sophistic form. Such a work is the *Epitaphius* of Lysias. This oration, following the fashion of such " show-speeches" (ἐπιδείξεις), goes through the historical and mythical ages, stringing together the great deeds of the Athenians in chronological order ; dwelling at great length on the mythical proofs of Athenian bravery and humanity, such as their war with the Amazons, their exer-tions in obtaining the sepulture of the heroes who fell at Thebes, and their reception of the Heracleidæ ; then recounting the exploits of the Athenians during the Persian invasion ; but passing rapidly over the Peloponnesian war ;—in direct contrast to the plan of Thucydides ;—and in general laying the greatest stress on those topics which were most adapted for panegyrical declamation. ‖ These ideas are worked out in so forced and artificial a manner, that we cannot wonder at those scholars who have failed to recognize in this speech the same Lysias that we find in the judicial orations. The whole essay is pervaded by a regular

* With the exception, as it seems, of the singular little speech, πρὸς τοὺς συνου-σιαστὰς κακολογιῶν, which is neither a judicial speech nor yet a mere μιλίτη. It seems to be based upon real occurrences, but is altogether sophistical in the execution. It is a tract in which Lysias renounces the friendship of those with whom he had been on terms of intimacy and friendship.

† συμβουλευτικὸν γένος, *deliberativum genus.*
‡ δικανικὸν, *judiciale genus.*　　　§ ἐπιδεικτικὸν, πανηγυρικὸν γένος.
‖ The only passage in which he evinces any real interest in his subject is that in which he extols those who put down the tyranny of the Thirty, and among them, the strangers who fought for the democracy on that occasion, and conse-quently obtained in death the same privileges as the citizens themselves (§ 66).

accused is the common enemy of the judges and of the accuser, the
procemium at once conciliates the good will of the judges. It draws the
attention of the audience to a highly interesting narrative, in which the
fall of the democracy is connected with the ruin of Dionysodorus, whom
the accuser seeks to avenge. This narrative, which at the same time
unfolds the state of the case, and is premised as the main point in
it,* begins with the battle of Ægos-potami, and details all the detestable
manœuvres by which Theramenes endeavoured to deliver up his native
city, unarmed, into the power of her enemies. The fear of Theramenes
lest the leaders of the army should detect and thwart his intrigues, led
to the guilt of Agoratus: according to the orator's account of the matter,
Agoratus willingly undertook to represent the commanders as enemies
of the peace, in consequence of which they were apprehended and
judicially murdered by the Council under the Thirty Tyrants. This
narrative, which is given in the most vivid colours, and, in its main
features, is supported by evidence, concludes, with the same artful and
well-contrived simplicity which reigns throughout the speech, in a scene
in the dungeon, where Dionysodorus, after disposing of his property,
leaves it as a sacred duty to be performed by his brother and brother-in-
law, the accuser, and all his friends, nay, even by his unborn child, that
they should take vengeance for his death on Agoratus, who, according to
the Athenian way of viewing the matter, was considered as the chief author
of it. The accuser now briefly sketches the mischiefs done by the
Thirty—who could not have got their power without the intrigues here
referred to; confutes some pleas which Agoratus might bring forward in
his justification, by a careful scrutiny of all the circumstances attending
his denunciation; then enlarges upon the whole life of Agoratus; the
meanness of his family, his usurpation of the rights of citizenship, his
dealings with the liberators at Phyle, with whom he sought to identify
himself,† but was rejected by them as a murderer; then justifies the
harsh measure of the summary process (ἀπαγωγή), which the accuser
had thought fit to employ against Agoratus; and finally proves, that the
amnesty between the two parties at Athens did not apply to Agoratus.
The epilogue very emphatically lays before the judges the dilemma in
which they were placed, of either condemning Agoratus, or justifying the
execution of those persons whose ruin he had effected. The excellence
of this brief but weighty speech will be perceived even from this

* The διήγησις is elsewhere used by Lysias as the κατάστασις, or definition of the
status causæ, and immediately follows the exordium; whereas Antiphon follows up
the exordium, without the introduction of any κατάστασις, by a part of the proofs,
e. g. the direct proof or formal nullification, and then at last introduces the διήγησις
to pave the way for other proofs, such as those springing from probability.
† Here an obscure point remains to be settled—what induced Agoratus to join
the exiles at Phyle? The orator gives no reason for this conduct, but only adduces
it as a proof of his shameless impudence, § 77.

summary of it: it lies open to only one censure, which is generally brought against Lysias by the old rhetoricians—that the proofs of his accusation, which follow the narrative, hang together too loosely, and have not the unity which might easily have been produced by a more accurate attention to a closer connexion of thought.

§ 6. Lysias was, in these and the following years, wonderfully prolific as an orator. The ancients were acquainted with 425 orations which passed under his name; of these, 250 are recognized as genuine: we have 35 of them, which, by the order in which they have come down to us, appear to have belonged to two separate collections.* One of these collections originally comprised all the speeches of Lysias arranged according to the causes pleaded in them, a principle of arrangement which we have already discovered in the case of Antiphon. Of this collection we have but a mere fragment, containing the last of the speeches on manslaughter, the speeches about impiety, and the first of the speeches about injuries:† either from accident or from caprice, the Funeral Oration is placed among these. The second collection begins with the important speech against Eratosthenes. It contains no complete class of speeches, but is clearly a selection from the works of Lysias, the choice of speeches being guided by their historical interest. Consequently, a considerable number of these speeches carry us deeply into the history of the time before and after the tyranny of the Thirty, and are among the most important authorities for the events of this period with which we are not sufficiently acquainted from other sources. As might be expected, none of these speeches is anterior in date to the speech against Eratosthenes:‡ nor can we show that any one of them is subsequent to Ol. 98, 2. B.C. 387, § although Lysias is said to have lived till Ol. 100, 2 or 3. B.C. 378. ‖ The arrangement is neither chronological, nor according to the causes pleaded; but is an arbitrary compound of both.

---

* According to the discovery made by a young friend of the Author, which will probably be soon brought out in a complete and finished state.

† The speech for Eratosthenes is an ἀπολογία φονοῦ, and is followed by the speech against Simon, and the following περὶ τραύματος, which also belong to the φονικοὶ λόγοι; then come the speeches περὶ ἀσιβίας, for Callias, against Andocides, and about the Olive: then follow the speeches κακολογιῶν, to his comrades, for the warriors, and against Theomnestus. The speech about the Olive is cited by Harpocration, v. σηκός, as contained ἐν τοῖς τῆς ἀσιβίας, and so his τῶν συμβολαίων λόγοι, ἐπιτροπικοὶ λόγοι, are also quoted.

‡ The speech of Polystratus does not belong to the time of the Four-hundred, but was delivered at the scrutiny (δοκιμασία) which Polystratus had to undergo as an officer of his tribe, and at which he was charged with having belonged to the Four-hundred. The speech δήμου καταλύσεως ἀπολογία was delivered under similar circumstances.

§ The speech about the property of Aristophanes probably falls under this year.

‖ A speech in the first series (that against Theomnestus) was written later,— Ol. 98, 4, or 99, 1. B.C. 384.

CHAPTER XXXVI.

§ 1. Early training of Isocrates; but slightly influenced by Socrates. § 2. School of Isocrates; its great repute; his attempts to influence the politics of the day without thoroughly understanding them. § 3. The form of a speech the principal matter in his judgment. § 4. New developement which he gave to prose composition. § 5. His structure of periods. § 6. Smoothness and evenness of his style. § 7. He prefers the panegyrical oratory to the forensic.

§ 1. It is very doubtful whether Plato would have accorded to Isocrates in his maturer age those high praises which he has bestowed upon him in the earlier years of his life, or would have preferred him so decidedly to Lysias. Isocrates, the son of Theodorus, was born at Athens in Ol. 86, 1. B.C. 436, and was, consequently, about 24 years younger than Lysias. He was, no doubt, a well-conducted youth, eager to acquire information; and, to get himself thoroughly educated, became a pupil, not only of the Sophists Gorgias and Tisias, but also of Socrates. In the circle of his friends so strong an impression was created in his favour, that it was believed that " he would not only in oratory leave all other orators behind him like children, but that a divine instinct would lead him on to still greater things. For that there was an earnest love of wisdom in the heart of the man." Such is the prophecy concerning him which Plato puts into the mouth of Socrates himself. Notwithstanding this, however, Isocrates seems to have made no use of the great philosopher beyond acquiring from him such a superficial knowledge of moral philosophy as would enable him to give a colouring of science to his professional exertions. Rhetoric was, after all, his main occupation, and no age before his had seen so much care and labour expended on this art. Accordingly, Isocrates essentially belongs to the Sophists, differing from them only in this, that he could not any longer oppose the Socratic philosophy by the bold proposal of making all things equally true by argument:* on the contrary, he considered speech as only a means of setting forth, in as pleasing and brilliant a manner as possible, some opinion, which, though not very profound, was, at any rate, quite praiseworthy in itself. If, however, he was less concerned about enlarging his ideas and getting a deeper insight into the reality of things, or, in general, comprehending the truth with greater clearness and accuracy, than about perfecting the outward form and ornamental finish of his

---

* See the speech περὶ ἀντιδόσεως, § 30, where he justly repudiates the charge, that he was corrupting the youth by teaching them to turn right into wrong in the courts of justice. Comp. § 15.

style, it follows that Plato, if he had criticized him when farther advanced in his career, must have classed him among the artizans, who strove after a mere semblance of truth, in opposition to the true philosophers.

§ 2. Isocrates had a strong desire to give a political turn to the art of speaking which, with the exception of the panegyrical species, had hitherto been cultivated chiefly for the contests of the courts :* but bashfulness and physical weakness prevented him from ascending himself the bema in the Pnyx. Consequently, he set up a school, in which he principally taught political oratory ; and so sedulously did he instruct young men in rhetoric, that his industry was fully recognized by his contemporaries, and his school became the first and most flourishing in Greece.† Cicero compares this school to the wooden horse of the Trojan war, because a similar number of oratorical heroes proceeded from it. Public speakers and historians were his principal auditors; and the reason of this was, that Isocrates always selected for his exercises such practical subjects as appeared to him both profitable and dignified, and chiefly proposed as a study to his hearers the political events of his own time—a circumstance which he has himself alleged as the main distinction between himself and the Sophists. ‡ The orations which Isocrates composed were mostly destined for the school; the law-speeches which he wrote for actual use in the courts were merely a secondary consideration. However, after the name of Isocrates had become famous, and the circle of his scholars and friends extended over all the countries inhabited by Greeks, Isocrates calculated upon a more extended publicity for many of his orations than his school would have furnished, and especially for those which touched on the public transactions of Greece : and their literary circulation, by means of copies and recitations, obtained for him a wider influence than a public delivery from the bema would have done. In this manner, Isocrates might, even from the recesses of his school, have produced a beneficial effect on his native land, which, torn with internal discord, was striving against the powerful Macedonian ; and, to say the truth, we cannot but allow that there is an effort to attain this great object in those literary productions which he addressed, at different times, to the Greeks in general, to the Athenians, to Philip, or to still remoter princes ;§ nay, we some-

* τὸ δικανικὸν γίνος. Isocrates, in his speech against the Sophists, § 19, blames earlier rhetoricians for making the δικάζεσθαι the chief point, and so bringing forward the least agreeable side of rhetoric.

† He soon had about 100 hearers, each of whom paid a fee of 1000 drachmæ (one-sixth of a talent).

‡ See especially the panegyric on Helen, § 5, 6.

§ In this manner Isocrates endeavoured to work upon the island of Cyprus, where at that time the Greek state of Salamis had raised itself into importance. His *Evagoras* is a panegyric on that excellent ruler, addressed to his son and successor, Nicocles. The tract *Nicocles* is an exhortation to the Salaminians to

times find in them a certain amount of plain-speaking ;* but it is quite
clear that Isocrates had none of those profound views of policy which
could alone have given weight and efficiency to his suggestions. He
shows the very best intentions, always exhorts to concord and peace, lives
in the hope that every state will give up its extravagant claims, set free
its dependent allies, and place itself on an equal footing with them, and
that, in consequence of these happy changes, something great will be
undertaken against the barbarians. We find nowhere in Isocrates any
clear and well-based conception of the principles by which Greece may be
guided to this golden age of unity and concord, especially of the rights of the
states which would be affected by it, and the claims which would have to
be set aside. In the speech about the peace, which was published during
the Social War, he advises the Athenians, in the first part, to grant independence to the rebellious islanders ; in the second part, he recommends
them to give up their maritime supremacy—judicious and excellent propo-
sals, which would only have the effect of annihilating the power of Athens
and checking every tendency to manly exertion. In his *Areopagiticus*
he declares that he sees no safety for Athens, save in the restoration of
that democracy which Solon had founded and Cleisthenes had revived ;
as if it were possible to restore, without the least trouble in the world,
a constitution, which, in the course of time, had undergone such manifold
changes, and, with it, the old simplicity of manner, which had altogether
disappeared. In his *Panegyricus*, he exhorts all the Greeks to give up
their animosities, and to direct their ambition against the barbarians ;
the two chief states, Athens and Sparta, having so arranged as to divide
the Hegemony or leadership between them : a plan very sensible at the
time, and not altogether impracticable, but requiring a totally different
basis from that which Isocrates lays down ; for presuming a violent
objection on the part of the Lacedæmonians, he proves to them, from
the mythical history of early times, that Athens was more deserving of the
leadership than Sparta. † The only true and correctly conceived part of
the speech is that in which he displays the divided condition of Greece,
and the facility with which the Greeks, if only united, could make con-
quests in Asia. Lastly, in his *Philip*, a tract inscribed to the king of
Macedon, when this prince, in consequence of the treaty concluded by

obey their new ruler ; and his harangue *to Nicocles* is an exhortation addressed to
the young ruler, on the duties and virtues of a sovereign.

* " I am accustomed to write my orations with plainness of speech," says he
in his letter to Archidamus (IX.), § 13. This letter is undoubtedly genuine ; but
the following, that to Dionysius (X.), is, as clearly, the work of a later rhetorician
of the Asiatic school.

† What Isocrates says in this speech (written about Ol. 100, 1. B.C. 380): τὴν
μὲν ἡμετέραν πόλιν ῥᾴδιον ἐπὶ ταῦτα προαγαγών, at all events does not accord with the
result of the negotiations given in Xenoph., *Hellen.* VI. 5, § 3, 4 ; VII. 1, § 8 and
14 (Ol. 102, 4. B.C. 369) ; where Athens renounces the only practical method of
sharing the Hegemony, by land and water, which the Lacedæmonians had offered.

Æschines, had placed Athens in a disagreeable predicament, he exhorts the Macedonian to come forward as mediator between the dissident states of Greece—the wolf as mediator in the quarrels of the sheep—and then to march along with their united forces against the Persians—the very thing which Philip wished to do, but then he desired to do so in the only possible way by which it could be brought about, namely, as their leader, and, under this name, as the ruler of the free states of Greece.

How strange, then, must have been the feelings of Isocrates, when news was brought to him of the downfal of Athenian power and Greek independence at Chæronea! His benevolent hopes must have been so rudely dashed to the ground by this one stroke, that probably it was disappointment, no less than patriotic grief for the loss of freedom, that induced him to put an end to his life.

§ 3. The manner in which he speaks of them himself makes it evident that his heart was but little affected by the subjects treated of in these speeches. In his *Philip* he mentions that he had treated on the same theme—the exhortation to the Greeks to unite themselves against the barbarians—in his *Panegyricus* also, and dwells on the difficulty of discussing the same subject in two different orations; " especially since," to use his own words, " the first published is so accurately composed that even our detractors imitate it, and tacitly admire it more than those who praise it most extravagantly." * In the *Panathenaicus*, an eulogium on Athens, written by Isocrates when far advanced in age, he says, that he had given up all earlier kinds of rhetoric, and had devoted himself to the composition of speeches which concerned the welfare of the city and of Greece in general; and, consequently, had composed discourses " full of thoughts, and decked out with not a few antitheses and parisoses, and those other figures which shine forth in the schools of rhetoric and compel the hearers to signify their applause by shouting and clapping;" at the present time, however, being 94 years old, he did not think it becoming in him to use this style, but would speak as every one thought himself capable of speaking if he chose, though no one would be able to do so who had not bestowed upon his style the necessary attention and labour.† It is clear, that, while Isocrates pretends to be casting his glance over all Europe and Asia, and to have his soul filled with anxiety for his native land, the object which he really has in his eye is the approbation of the school and the triumph of his art over all rivals. So that, after all, these great panegyrical orations belong to the class of school-rhetoric, no less than the *Praise of Helen* and the *Busiris*, which Isocrates composed immediately after the pattern of the Sophists, who frequently selected mythical subjects for their encomiastic or vituperative

* Isocrat. *Philipp.*, § 11. See the similar assertion in the *Panegyricus* itself, § 4.
† Isocrat. *Panathen.*, § 2.

discourses. In the *Praise of Helen* he blames another rhetorician
for writing a defence of this much maligned heroine, after having
professed to write her eulogium. In the *Busiris* he shows the Sophist
Polycrates how he should have drawn up his encomium of this bar-
barous tyrant, and also incidentally sets him right with regard to an
ill selected topic which he had introduced into an accusation of Socrates,
composed by him as a sophistical exercise. Polycrates had given
Socrates the credit of educating Alcibiades; " a fact which no one had
remarked, but which redounded rather to the credit than to the discredit
of Socrates, seeing that Alcibiades had so far excelled all other men." *
In this passage Isocrates merely criticizes Polycrates for an injudicious
choice of topics, without expressing any opinion upon the character of
Socrates, or the justice of his sentence; which were considerations
foreign to the question. Isocrates attempts to pass off his own rhetorical
studies for philosophy,† but he really had very little acquaintance with
the philosophical strivings of his age. Otherwise he would not have
included in one class, as " the contentious philosophers," the Eleatics
Zeno and Melissus, whose sole object was to discover the truth, and the
Sophists Protagoras and Gorgias. ‡

§ 4. Little as we may be disposed, after all these strictures, to regard
Isocrates as a great statesman or philosopher, he is not only eminent, but
constitutes an epoch in himself, as a rhetorician or artist of language.
Over and above the great care which he took about the formation of his
style, Isocrates had a decided genius for the art of rhetoric; and, when
we read his periods, we may well believe what he tells us, that the
Athenians, alive as they were to beauties of this kind, felt a real enthusiasm for his writings, and friends and enemies vied in imitating their
magic elegance. When we read aloud the panegyrical orations of
Isocrates, we feel that, although they want the vigour and profundity
of Thucydides or Aristotle, there is a power in them which we miss
in every former work of rhetoric—a power which works upon the mind
as well as upon the ear; we are carried along by a full stream of harmonious diction, which is strikingly different from the rugged sentences
of Thucydides and the meagre style of Lysias. The services which
Isocrates has performed in this respect reach far beyond the limits of his
own school. Without his reconstruction of the style of Attic oratory
we could have had no Demosthenes and no Cicero; and, through these,

* *Busiris,* § 5.
† *e. g.* in the speech to *Demonicus,* § 3; *Nicocles,* § 1; *Concerning the Peace,* § 5;
Busiris, § 7; *Against the Sophists,* § 14; *Panathenaicus,* § 263. In his περὶ ἀντιδόσεως, § 30, he opposes the περὶ τὰς δίκας καλινδούμενου to the περὶ τὴν φιλοσοφίαν
διατρίψαντις.
‡ *Praise of Helen,* § 2—6: ἡ περὶ τὰς ἔριδας φιλοσοφία. Similarly in the speech
περὶ ἀντιδόσεως, § 268, he mixes up the physical speculations of the Eleatics and
Pythagoreans with the sophisms of Gorgias.

the school of Isocrates has extended its influence even to the oratory of our own day.

Isocrates started from the style which had been most cultivated up to his time, namely, the antithetical.* In his earlier labours he took as much pains with this symmetrical structure as any Sophist could have done: but in the more flourishing period of his art he contrived to melt down the rigidity and stiffness of the antithesis, by breaking through the direct and immediate opposition of sentences, and by marshalling them in successive groups and in a longer series.

Isocrates has always one leading idea, which is in most cases of suitable importance, fertile in its consequences, and capable of evoking not only thought but feeling; hence his fondness for general political subjects, which furnished him best with such topics. In these leading thoughts he seizes certain points opposed to one another, such as the old and the new times, or the power of the Greeks and that of the barbarians; and expanding the leading idea in a regular series of sequences and conclusions, he introduces at every step in the composition the propositions which contradict it in its details, and in this way unfolds an abundance of variations always pervaded and marked by a recurrence of the original subject; so that, although there is great variety, the whole may be comprehended at one glance. At the same time, Isocrates is careful that the ear may be cognizant of the antitheses which are presented to the thoughts, and he manages this after the fashion of the older Sophists: but he differs from them, partly in not caring so much about the assonances of individual words, as about the rhythm of whole sentences; partly by seeking to break up the more exact correspondence of sentences into a system less marked by the stiff regularity of its members; and partly by introducing into the longer sets of antithetical sentences a gradual increase in the force and intensity of his language; this he effected by extending the sentences, especially in the third member and at the end; † and thus an entirely new vigour of movement was given to the old antithetical construction.

§ 5. The ancients recognize Isocrates as the author or first introducer of the *circle of language*, as it was called,‡ although the Sophist Thrasymachus, a contemporary of Antiphon, is acknowledged to have been master of "the diction which concentrates the ideas and expresses them roundly." ‡ It was the same Thrasymachus whose chief aim it was

---

* ἀντικειμένη λέξις.

† "In composite sentences," says Demetrius, *de Elocut.*, § 18, "the last member must be longer than the others."   ‡ κύκλος, *orbis orationis.*

‡ ἡ συστρέφουσα τὰ διανοήματα καὶ στρογγύλως ἐκφέρουσα λέξις. See Theophrastus (*apud Dionys. de Lys. judic.*, p. 464), who lays claim to this art on behalf of Lysias also. What is meant by the στρογγύλον appears clearly from the example which Hermogenes (Walz. *Rhetores* III., p. 704) has given from Demosthenes: ὥσπερ γὰρ, εἴτις ἐκείνων ἑάλω, σὺ τάδε οὐκ ἂν ἔγραψας· οὕτως, ἂν σὺ νῦν ἁλῷς, ἄλλος οὐ γράψει. Such a sentence is like a circle which necessarily returns to itself.

to have the power of either rousing or quieting the anger of his hearers
(*e. g.* the judges), and, in general, of working at pleasure on the feelings
of men.   There was a work of his called " The Commiseration Speeches"
(ἔλεοι), and it is to be remarked that this tendency of his eloquence must
have induced him at the same time to give an easier and more lively flow
to his sentences.   It was Isocrates, however, above all others, who, by a
judicious choice of subjects, imparted to his language the harmonious
effect which is so closely connected with the *circle of language*, as it is
called.   By this we understand such a formation and distribution of the
periods that the several members follow one another as integral parts
of one whole, and the general conclusion is expected by the hearer in the
very place where it occurs, and is, as it were, almost heard before it is
uttered.*   This impression is produced partly by the union of the
several sentences in larger masses, partly by the relation of these masses
to one another, so that, without counting or measuring, we feel that there
is a sort of harmony which a little, either more or less, would utterly
destroy.   This is not merely true of primary and subordinate sentences,
in the proper sense of the word, which are mutually developed by the
logical subordination of thoughts to one another,† but also holds of the
co-ordinate masses of opposed sentences (in that antithetical style ‡ to
which Isocrates' longer periods mostly belong), if a periodical cadence
is introduced into them.   The ancients themselves compare a period in
which there is a true equilibrium of all parts with a dome § in which all
the stones tend with equal weight to the middle point.   It is obvious that
this must be regulated by the rhetorical accent, which is the same in oratory
that the grammatical accents are in language, and the *arsis* and *thesis* in
rhythm : these accents must regularly correspond to one another, and
each fully occupy its own place : an improper omission, and especially a
loss of the fuller accent at the end of the period, is most sensibly felt by
a fine and correct ear.   The ancients, however, like the moderns, rather
leave this main point to be fixed by a sort of general feeling, and reserve
definite rules for the subordinate details, upon which Isocrates has bestowed most extraordinary pains in his panegyrical speeches.   Euphonious
combinations of sound, avoidance of hiatus, certain rhythmical feet at the
beginning and end of sentences, these are the objects which he aims at
with labour far more than proportioned to the effects which they produce
on the hearer.   This sort of prose has, in these particulars, a great
resemblance to tragedy, which also avoided the hiatus more than any
other kind of poetic composition.‖

---

* Compare Cicero's admirable remarks, *Orator.* 53, 177, 178.
† Such as temporal, causal, conditional, and concessive protases, with their
apodoses.
‡ ἀντικειμένη λέξις.   § περιφερὴς στίγη.
‖ The ancients frequently express their well-founded opinion, that the juxta-
position of vowels in words and collocations of words produces a soft (*molle quid-*

§ 6. Isocrates was justly impressed with the necessity of having a certain class of subjects for the developement of this particular style. He is accustomed to combine the substance and form of his oratory, as when he reckons himself among those " who wrote no speeches about private matters, but Hellenic, political, and panegyrical orations, which, as all persons must allow, are more nearly akin to the musical and metrical language of the poets than to those speeches which are heard in the law-courts."* The full stream of Isocratic diction necessitates the recurrence of certain leading ideas, such as are capable of being brought out in the details with the greatest possible variety, and of being proved by a continually increasing weight of conviction. The predominance of the rhetoric of Isocrates consequently banished from the Attic style more and more of that subtilty and acuteness which seeks to give a definite and accurate expression to every idea, and to obtain this object a sacrifice was made of the correspondence of expressions, grammatical forms, and connexions of sentences, which formed the basis of that impressive and significant abruptness of diction by which the style of Sophocles and Thucydides is distinguished. The flowing language and long periods of Isocrates, if they had had any of this abruptness, would have lost that intelligibility without which the hearers would not have been able to foresee what was coming, and to feel the gratification resulting from a fulfilment of their expectations. In Thucydides, on the contrary, we can scarcely feel confident of having seized the meaning even when we get to the end of the sentence. Hence it is that Isocrates has avoided all those finer distinctions which vary the grammatical expression. His object manifestly is to continue as long as possible the same structure with the same case, mood, and tense. The language of Isocrates, however, though pervaded by a certain genial warmth of feeling, is quite free from the influence of those violent emotions, which, when combined with a shrewdness and cunning foreign to the candid disposition of Isocrates, produce the so-called figures of thought.† Accordingly, though we find in his speeches vehement questions, exclamations, and climaxes, we have none of those stronger and more irregular changes of the expression which such figures beget. Isocrates also seeks a rhythmical structure of periods, which seldom admits of any relation of the sentences calculated to cause sur-

---

dam, Cicero) and melodious effect (μέλος, is the expression of Demetrius), such as was suitable to epic poetry and the old Ionic prose. The contraction and elision of vowels, on the other hand, make language more plain and compact ; and, when all collisions of vowels at the end and beginning of words is avoided, a kind of smoothness and finish is produced, such as was necessary for dramatic poetry and panegyrical oratory. According to Dionysius, every hiatus is removed from the *Areopagiticus* of Isocrates ; to produce this, however, there must have been a greater number of Attic contractions (*crases*) than we find in the present state of the text.

* Isocrates, περὶ ἀντιδόσεως, § 46.
† σχήματα τῆς διανοίας, Chap. XXXIII., § 5.

prise by their inequality : * he aims at an equability of tone, or at least
a tranquillity of feeling; deep and varied emotions would necessarily
break the bonds of these regular periods, and combine the scattered
members in a new and bolder organization. The ancients, therefore,
agree that Isocrates was entirely deficient in that *vehemence of oratory*
which transfers the feelings of the speaker to his audience, and which is
called δεινότης in the narrower sense of the word ; not so much because
the labour of polishing the style in its minor details mars this vigour of
speech (as Plutarch says of Isocrates: " How could he help fearing the
charge of the phalanx, who was so afraid of allowing one vowel to come
in contact with another, or of giving the *isocolon* one syllable less than
it ought to have," †), but because this smoothness and evenness of style
depended for its very existence upon a tranquil train of thoughts, with
no perturbations of feeling to distract the even tenor of its way.

§ 7. In the well-founded conviction that his style was peculiarly
adapted to panegyrical eloquence, Isocrates rarely employed it in
forensic speeches ; in these he approximates more nearly to Lysias.
However, he was not, like the orator just mentioned, a professed speech-
writer, or *logographus*. The writers of speeches for the law-courts
appeared to him, as compared with his pursuits, to be only doll-makers
as compared with Phidias ; ‡ he wrote comparatively few speeches for
private persons and for practical purposes. The collection which has
come down to us, and which comprises the majority of the speeches
recognized by the ancients as the genuine works of Isocrates, § contains 15 admonitory, panegyrical, and scholastic discourses, which were all
designed for private perusal, and not for popular assemblies or law-
courts ; and after these come six forensic orations, which, no doubt, were
written for actual delivery in a court of justice. ‖ Isocrates also wrote,

* As in the beautiful antithetic period at the beginning of the *Panathenaicus*,
the first part of which, with the μίν, is very artificially divided by the opposition
of negation and position, and the developement of the negation in particular by
the insertion of concessive sentences ; while the second part is broken off quite
short. If we express the scheme of the period thus :—

A..........B
I   II
a, α, b, β, g, γ   a b

B consists only of the words νῦν δ' οὐδ' ὁπωσοῦν τοὺς τοιούτους. In this Isocrates may
have imitated Demosthenes.

† Plutarch, *de gloria Athen.*, c. VIII. Demetrius (*de Elocut.*, § 247) remarks,
that antitheses and paromœa are not compatible with δεινότης.

‡ περὶ ἀντιδόσεως, § 2.

§ Cæcilius acknowledged as genuine only 28 speeches. We have 21.

‖ The speech about the exchange (περὶ ἀντιδόσεως) does not belong to this class.
It is not a forensic speech, but written when Isocrates was compelled by the offer
of an exchange to sustain a most expensive liturgy,—the Trierarchy. In order to
correct the false impressions which were entertained with regard to his profession
and income, he *wrote* this speech as " a picture of his whole life, and of the plan
which he had pursued," § 7.

at a later period, a theoretical treatise, or τέχνη, embodying the principles which he had followed in his teaching, and which he had improved and worked out by practice. This work was much esteemed by ancient rhetoricians, and is often quoted. *

We have now brought the history of Attic prose, through a series of statesmen, orators, and rhetoricians, from Pericles to Isocrates : we have not yet arrived at its highest point; but still this was a remarkable eminence. We now go back again for a few years, in order to commence from a new beginning, not only of Attic training, but of the human mind in general, and to take under consideration a series of remarkable appearances springing from that source.

CHAPTER XXXVII.

§ 1. Socrates; his literary importance. § 2. Aristocratic tendency of Athenian literature during the Peloponnesian war. § 3. Subjectivity of the Socratic school. § 4. Imperfect Socratic schools; Aristippus and the Cyrenaics, as contrasted with, § 5. Antisthenes and the Cynics.

§ 1. ALTHOUGH Socrates left no writings behind him, and perhaps does not, strictly speaking, deserve a place among the contributors to Greek literature, yet when we consider that the history of a nation's literature is the history also of their intellectual developement; when we reflect how the intellect of Greece was affected by an extension of the principles of Socratic philosophy, and especially when we remember that the greatest literary genius that ever appeared in Greece owed much, if not most, of his mental training to his early intercourse with Socrates, we cannot well proceed any further in our inquiries without bestowing a few pages on this great master, and the minor schools of philosophy which claimed him as their head.

Socrates, the son of Sophroniscus, an Athenian sculptor, and of Phæ-narete, a midwife, was born in Ol. 78, 1. B.C. 468. He was brought up to his father's profession, which he practised with some success, though he did not by any means make it his principal occupation. A strong natural tendency to philosophical speculation, fostered and encouraged by frequent opportunities of intercourse with the eminent teachers of the day, soon drew him away to more congenial pursuits, and he became known, at an early period, as one devoted to the acquirement of know-

* The most important citation from it is that contained in a scholiast on Hermogenes. See Spengel, Συναγωγὴ τιχνῶν, p. 161.

ledge, and not only willing, but eager, to converse with any one on those subjects which were considered most interesting to the original thinkers of his day. Though strongly opposed to the tenets of Protagoras and Gorgias, he was regarded by many of his countrymen as one of the same class of speculators; Aristophanes represents him as a mischievous innovator in education; and, many years afterwards, Æschines did not hesitate to speak of him as " Socrates the Sophist."[*] After having served his country as a soldier during the Peloponnesian war, and having survived the frightful anarchy which succeeded that struggle between democracy and oligarchy, he was, shortly after the restoration of the old constitution at Athens, brought to trial, charged with impiety and with corrupting the minds of the rising generation; and, partly in consequence of his own proud and unbending demeanour at the trial, was sentenced to death, and condemned to drink the cup of hemlock, in Ol. 95, 2., B.C. 399.

The circumstances which led to this catastrophe are, after all, those which render Socrates most particularly an object of interest in a literary point of view. We are not so much concerned about establishing the excellence of his moral character, or vindicating his claim to the first place in Greek philosophy, as about clearly understanding and explaining his influence on the literature of Greece as it appeared after his time.

§ 2. If we were asked what constituted the difference between the Greek literature of the fifth century B.C. and that of the preceding ages, we should, perhaps, be justified in answering, that literature was Hellenic before that time, but that during the fifth century it became more and more exclusively Athenian. During this period almost every branch of literature was cultivated at Athens to a much greater extent than in all the rest of Greece: the drama was peculiarly her own; oratory was nowhere so powerful as in the Pnyx; the Attic prose style was a model for every Greek writer; philosophy, whether native or foreign, flourished only by the banks of the Ilissus; and, in every sense, Athens was the Prytaneum of Greek wisdom,[†] where the central fire blazed on its own altar, ministering, however, light and warmth to all the lands of Greece. Yet, though this great Attic literature had sprung up in the midst of democracy, and would, no doubt, have been checked in its free developement by any other form of government, it contained within itself a principle of antagonism which soon placed it in open opposition to that very political freedom in which it took its rise. In order to investigate what this principle was we must enter somewhat more deeply into the subject.

* Æschines, c. Timarch., p. 24: ἴστε δ᾽ ὑμεῖς, ὦ Ἀθηναῖοι, Σωκράτην τὸν σοφιστὴν ἀπεκτείνατε.
† Plato, Protagoras, p. 337 c.: συνεληλυθότας τῆς Ἑλλάδος εἰς αὐτὸ τὸ πρυτανεῖον τῆς σοφίας.

When literary exertions are occasioned by something in the state of a country—its religion or its political constitution—as when the worship of Bacchus gave rise to the drama, or, more generally, the worship of Apollo produced some species or other of choral lyric poetry, or when the democratic constitutions of Greece created a school of oratory,—we may remark, that a conviction of the importance of the object in view stifles all literary vanity, and the poet is more apt to exult in the thought that he is a minister of the god, than to take pride in the efforts of his genius. As time, however, wears on, the business of the bard becomes more and more professional; he begins to feel conscious of his own importance, and communicates this sentiment to others, till, at last, the writer of the song or hymn is more in the thoughts of his readers and hearers, than the deity in whose honour he has composed the poem. We remark something of this even in Pindar. But the tendency is more strikingly shown in the cultivation of prose. From the first beginning of artificial prose, in the time of the Sophists, down to its perfection by Isocrates, we have seen that its prevailing feature is a consciousness of skill. From this consciousness of skill, or the power of doing what others cannot do so well, another feeling immediately results, namely, a sense of superiority in the exclusive possession of art. Hence the literary man feels himself professional, or belonging to a class, in contradistinction to which all others are mere private individuals, or ἰδιῶται, as they were somewhat contemptuously called, and at last literature, which was the type and the product of free democratical Athens, becomes aristocratic and exclusive.

This tendency developed itself more especially during the Peloponnesian war, which may be defined to have been the great critical struggle between the democratic and aristocratic parties in Greece. It was while Athens was outwardly contending against the aristocracy of birth, that this aristocracy of talent sprung up within her walls. The name by which the oligarchical party all over Greece delighted to be called—καλοκἀγαθοί—properly implied education or accomplishment, as well as birth.* With the literary aristocrats of Athens the case was quite otherwise. Their principal renown was to be the pre-eminently καλοί, or " accomplished," and they cared little or nothing for the distinctions of birth. They felt that they constituted, as, in fact, they did, a sort of middle class, * whose interests were identical neither with those of the old nobles nor with those of the democracy. It would be difficult to name any very prominent literary man of this æra, with the single exception of Aristophanes, who did not belong to the literary aristocrats. Euripides, whose connexion with Socrates has long been sufficiently

---

* That is to say, they were neither τὸ φαῦλον, " the illiterate," nor τὸ πάνυ ἀκριβὲς, " the minute philosophers" (Thucyd. VI. 18). For φαῦλος as an epithet of the common people, see Eurip., Bacchæ 431 ; Æschin., c. Ctesiph., p. 65, 1.

understood, expressly declares, that of the three classes in the state the middle one saves the city;* Sophocles was one of the πρόβουλοι, or commissioners, who were selected as agents in the middle-class movement which preceded the oligarchy at Athens;† and Thucydides does not hesitate to say, that, in his opinion, this movement, which is generally known as the government of the Five-thousand, was the first good constitution which the Athenians had enjoyed in his time.‡ The political character who was at the head of this movement in favour of the middle classes was Theramenes, and all the hopes of those who conceived it possible to have a government of the καλοί, or educated men, without falling into oligarchy, rested upon this versatile and not very honest statesman. Critias, on the other hand, was for upholding the principles of the old oligarchies, and cared as little for the claims and interests of the middle classes as he did for those of the great mass of his fellow-citizens. This opposition between the parties of Critias and Theramenes appears to us to solve the whole problem as far as Socrates and his school are concerned. That Socrates disapproved of the views of Critias, § and would not contribute to carry out his nefarious measures for the aggrandizement of his party,‖ is established by the most express testimony. At the same time, he remained at Athens during the whole period of the anarchy, and never joined the patriots of Phyle. The inference from this is plain: he agreed with many and most of the principles of the educated party—the καλοί—and, upon the whole, preferred an aristocracy to the old constitution of his country; and, though he made a courageous effort to save the head of his party, Theramenes, from the vengeance of his great rival,¶ and would, no doubt, have contributed what he could to give a blow to the schemes of Critias and Charicles, he preferred his own Girondist theories to the democracy which succeeded the downfal of the oligarchs; and the knowledge of this, coupled with the belief that he was still a mischievous agent of the middle-class party, naturally induced Anytus, one of the leaders of the party of Thrasybulus, to indict him before the popular tribunal.

§ 3. These remarks on the political views of the literary party at Athens, of which Socrates was the head, were necessary to a right understanding of the new direction given to literature by Socrates and his school. It is well known that, as the speculations of the older philosophers, especially those of the Ionic school, were, for the most part confined to physics, and therefore treated only of the outer world,

---

* *Suppl.* 247: ἡμῶν δὲ μοιρῶν ἡ 'ν μέσῳ σῴζει πόλιν.
† Thucyd. VIII. 1.   Aristot., *Rhetor.* III. 18, § 6
‡ Thucyd. VIII. 97.   § Xenophon, *Mem.* I. 2, § 32.
‖ Plato, *Apologia Socr.*, p. 32, c.
¶ Diodor. Sic. XIV., c. 5: Σωκράτης δὲ ὁ φιλόσοφος καὶ δύο τῶν οἰκείων προσδραμόντες ἐπεχείρουν κωλύειν τοὺς ὑπηρέτας, ὁ δὲ Θηραμένης κ.τ.λ.

so the business of Socrates and his followers was chiefly with man himself, considered as a thinking subject; in other words, they were all, in some form or other, ethical philosophers.' The celebrated response of the Delphic oracle,—" Know thyself" (γνῶθι σεαντόν),—by which Socrates professed to be guided, was, in effect, the shortest conceivable expression of all his philosophical strivings. It has been well said by an eminent writer of our day, that the great service which Socrates rendered to philosophy was this, that he awakened the idea of science, or taught man to reflect on his own powers of thinking and knowing. Self-consciousness—knowing himself—and getting an acquaintance with his powers of knowing—this was from first to last the business of Socrates. With him knowing and doing were synonymous, since no man, according to his view of the case, could help doing what he knew to be right.* If, then, a man's morality or goodness varied with his knowledge, it followed that the καλοί, or men of education, were alone virtuous, and, by a natural consequence, alone fit to have the management of public affairs.† That such was the belief of the movement party at Athens is clear from the pains taken by Thrasybulus, in his first speech after the amnesty, to combat this notion.‡ This application of the Socratic doctrine of self-knowledge explains to us many of the more striking characteristics of the authors whose works we are about to examine. We see from this how it was that neither Xenophon nor Plato could tolerate the free democratic constitution of their country: we see, too, why they were both so anxious to promulgate theories on the principles of government: above all, we see how the literary man became professional, while, at the same time, he ceased to be a δημιουργὸς, or servant of the state which gave him birth, and wrote and thought for himself, for his own glory, and his own theories, without any regard to the patriotic or religious motives which were the main-spring of the older literature.

Before we enter upon a detailed examination of the writings of these two great Socratic writers, Xenophon and Plato, whose works have come down to us very nearly complete, and who, the one practically, the other theoretically, understood and carried out the true spirit of the teaching of Socrates, it will be advisable to take a brief view of the most important of these systems which proceeded upon a less perfect conception of the doctrines.

§ 4. In the later ages of Greek philosophy, by the side of the Academic and Peripatetic systems, which claimed as their founders a Socratic philosopher and his scholar, we seldom hear of any other schools but the Epicurean and the Stoic. We propose, in the remainder of this chapter, to show how these two may ultimately be traced to the teaching of Socrates.

* Aristot. *Eth. Eudem.* I. 5, § 13.   † Xenoph. *Mem.* III., 9, § 10.
‡ Xenoph. *Hellen.*, II. 4, § 39.

Among the pupils of Socrates was one who was regarded by his fellow-students as having but little sympathy with their master. This was ARISTIPPUS, a native of Cyrene, a man born of illustrious and wealthy parents, and brought up in luxury, but yet so far alive to subjects of philosophical interest, that he was induced, by the reports which he heard of Socrates,* to leave his home and become a pupil of the Athenian sage. He remained with his master until his execution, when he seems to have commenced a rambling life, till at length, in his old age, he returned to his native land, and there founded the so-called *Cyrenaic* school. The dialogues and other works attributed to him are entirely lost; but we are not without the means of forming a tolerably accurate opinion as to the tenets held by himself and his followers. He started from the Socratic doctrine of self-consciousness, but made a very different use of it from that which Socrates intended. The great business of man was, in his opinion, to learn and know what was most for his happiness; and in endeavouring to find out this, he came to the conclusion that pleasure was the true end of life. ' At the same time, he made a wide distinction between pleasure and the desire of pleasure. As all pleasures are similar, and none more desirable than another, men ought not to desire more than they already possess; and, though he did not preach abstinence, he maintained that every one ought to have the control over himself even in the midst of indulgence: the reason must keep its supremacy, and prescribe how far the body may give way to sensual gratifications. . He divided all ethical philosophy into five parts: (1) concerning things to be desired or avoided (περὶ τῶν αἱρετῶν καὶ φευκτῶν); (2) concerning affections (περὶ τῶν παθῶν); (3) concerning actions (περὶ τῶν πράξεων); (4) concerning causes (περὶ τῶν αἰτίων); and (5) concerning proofs (περὶ τῶν πίστεων). In the first of these, in opposition to the idea of the good, he probably insisted on the satisfaction which pleasure alone can furnish. In the second, he inculcated the doctrine that pain and pleasure are positive, and that neither of them is a mere negative. Pleasure is a gentle motion, like that of a ship carried on by a fair wind straight to the haven which its pilot seeks: pain is a violent motion, like that of a ship in a storm, when the vessel is not only in danger, but also driven out of its course, and prevented from attaining the object of its voyage: the state of indifference in which neither pleasure nor pain is felt, is likened to a calm, in which the ship stands still, and neither gains nor loses way.† The third part of the Cyrenaic system treated of the end of actions, maintaining with the Sophists that no action was in itself either good or bad, but that every action must be estimated by its results, *i.e.* according to the pleasure or pain which it procured for the agent. Philosophy, according to Aristippus, ought to give man a control over

---

* Sextus Empiricus *adv. Logicos*, viii., 2, p. 372.
† Diogen. Laërt. II., 86. Plato, *Philebus*, p. 42. E. Euseb. *Præpar. Ev.*, xiv. 18.

THE BIOGRAPHICAL DICTIONARY
OF THE
SOCIETY FOR THE DIFFUSION OF USEFUL KNOWLEDGE.

THE SOCIETY FOR THE DIFFUSION OF USEFUL KNOWLEDGE intends to publish a Complete Biographical Dictionary, which will appear in Quarterly half volumes: the first half volume was published the 1st of July, 1842.

A Biographical Dictionary, viewed as a whole, must not be compared with a selection of Biographies, such, for instance, as the Lives of Plutarch; nor, viewed in its parts, must it be compared with special Biography, which has always a particular object, and also a completeness unattainable in a work which professes to give, within reasonable limits, some account of all persons who have lived and have done any thing for which they ought to be remembered. A Biographical Dictionary is generally consulted as a ready means of getting sufficient information for the time, and as indicating the sources of further information.

The completeness which a Biographical Dictionary should aim at, consists in comprising the names of all persons who deserve a notice, and not in containing very elaborate lives of distinguished persons, and omitting those of little importance. Many names indeed are so conspicuous as to require a very particular notice, even in a Biographical Dictionary; others will require to be treated at some length, though within narrower limits: but there is a large class of persons obscurely known of whom a short notice will be sufficient. Such names are not unimportant, so far as they are connected with the history of any branch of knowledge or of any of the arts; yet to learn the little that can be known of them would often require a sacrifice of time and labour disproportionate to the value of the information, if a person had to make the search for himself. Such names peculiarly belong to a Biographical Dictionary; but it will often be sufficient to state the time of the birth and death, and the titles of the works of these persons, with the addition of a remark or two, wherever that can be done, which shall correctly characterize their labours.

A Biographical Dictionary may be used for the purpose of historical study, by selecting out of the alphabetical order the lives of men who were contemporary or in a certain relation of succession to one another, as political personages, teachers of philosophy, or kings of the same dynasty. With this view the last volume will contain tables of kings and other public personages, related to one another in the order of succession; and it will also contain synchronistic tables, exhibiting in their relations of time those personages who have had the chief influence on the course of human affairs and on the progress of knowledge.

Original sources will be examined whenever it can be done; at the end of each life, when it shall seem to be of sufficient importance, the authorities will be referred to; and in the case of writers, a list of their principal works will be given; or where a list might take up too much room, a reference will be given to some place where such list can be found. The initials of the name of each contributor to this work will be given at the end of the articles, and the names of the contributors in full in each volume.

This work is published by MESSRS. LONGMAN AND CO., quarterly, in Half-Volumes, containing between four and five hundred octavo pages, printed in double column. Each Half-Volume costs twelve shillings in boards; and one will appear at the beginning of January, April, July, and October. It is not possible to state precisely the number of Volumes of which the work will ultimately consist; but so far as the quantity can now be estimated, it will probably not exceed Thirty Volumes. There is also a Monthly issue of Parts containing one-third of the Half-Volume, price 4s. in a stiff wrapper.

UNDER THE SUPERINTENDENCE OF THE SOCIETY FOR THE
DIFFUSION OF USEFUL KNOWLEDGE.

In one volume, octavo, price 12s. cloth, or in two volumes, price 6s. 6d. each,

POLITICAL PHILOSOPHY.

THE FIRST PART, COMPRISING

PRELIMINARY DISCOURSE of the OBJECTS, PLEASURES, and
ADVANTAGES of POLITICAL SCIENCE.

PRINCIPLES OF GOVERNMENT.

ABSOLUTE MONARCHY—EASTERN DESPOTISMS.

EFFECTS OF ABSOLUTE MONARCHIES.

GOVERNMENTS OF CHINA AND JAPAN.

GOVERNMENT OF RUSSIA.

THE FEUDAL SYSTEM.

CONSTITUTIONAL MONARCHY.

THE FRENCH MONARCHY.

THE GERMANIC EMPIRE AND MONARCHIES.

THE ITALIAN MONARCHIES.

THE SPANISH AND PORTUGUESE MONARCHIES, and DANISH
AND SWEDISH MONARCHIES.

The Work may also be had in Twenty-two Numbers, price 6d. each.

Now publishing, to be completed in about Eight Monthly Parts,
price One Shilling each,

THE HORSE.

By WILLIAM YOUATT.

A New Edition, with Additions and Corrections; and an entirely New
Set of Cuts drawn by Mr. HARVEY.

London: CHAPMAN and HALL, 186, Strand.

London: Printed by WILLIAM CLOWES and SONS, Stamford Street.

Milton Keynes UK
Ingram Content Group UK Ltd.
UKHW010634211124
3018UKWH00048B/694

9 781146 143591